Keynes

Keynes

Useful Economics for the World Economy

Peter Temin and David Vines

The MIT Press
Cambridge, Massachusetts
London, England

MIT Press books may be purchased at special quantity discounts for business or sales promotional use. For information, email special_sales@mitpress.mit.edu.

Set in Sabon by the MIT Press. Printed and bound in the United States of America.

Library of Congress Cataloging-in-Publication Data

Temin, Peter.
Keynes : useful economics for the world economy / Peter Temin and David Vines.
    pages   cm
Includes bibliographical references and index.
ISBN 978-0-262-02831-8 (hardcover : alk. paper)
1. Keynes, John Maynard, 1883–1946. 2. Economists—Great Britain. 3. Economics—Great Britain—History—20th century. 4. Keynesian economics.
I. Vines, David. II. Title.
HB103.K47T49   2014
330.15'6—dc23
2014010637

10 9 8 7 6 5 4 3 2 1

for Charlotte and Jane

The long run is a misleading guide to current affairs. In the long run we are all dead. Economists set themselves too easy, too useless a task if in tempestuous seasons they can only tell us that when the storm is long past the ocean is flat again.

John Maynard Keynes, *A Tract on Monetary Reform* (1923), chapter 3

Contents

Preface

John Maynard Keynes was an intellectual giant of the twentieth century. He created a new branch of economics now known as macroeconomics, and he played a major role in the reconstruction of Europe and of the world economy after the Second World War. We have written this short introduction to Keynesian economics because his contributions are too often neglected. In addition, they are relegated to the understanding of a single economy; his contributions to an understanding of the global economy are ignored. In a time of global macroeconomic crisis, these insights are important.

This book provides a short survey of Keynesian economics that allows readers to apply its tools to current policy debates. The exposition is set within an account of Keynes' life that locates his innovations in historical time and place, describing economic thinking before Keynes to explain how difficult it was for him to escape from conventional wisdom. We set out the Keynesian analysis of a closed economy and expand the analysis to the international economy. We use only simple graphs and simple models, framed by brief narratives of the twentieth century and the early years of the twenty-first.

Keynesian economics came to be identified with the Great Depression and with the policies that were followed in the decades after the Second World War—a period now known as the golden age of economic growth. That extraordinary period came to an end in the 1970s. But after a period of crisis, we lived through another Keynesian age, with stable prices and active governments, from the early 1980s until 2008. That Keynesian age was brought to an end by a Global Financial Crisis.

As this book is being written, in the spring of 2014, our immediate problems threaten to derail our long-run goals. It is useful to recall Keynes' contributions because they can help us get back onto a favorable path of economic growth. We argue that Keynes was concerned with the world economy and with interactions between countries. Those concerns were central in his work from 1919, when he reacted to the Treaty of Versailles, until 1944, when he was instrumental in constructing the Bretton Woods system of international monetary management. And although Keynes focused on the short run (as our epigraph shows), his theories were complemented by a clear understanding of the process of long-run economic growth. These interrelated aspects of Keynes' insights can help us today in a global economy.

This book explains basic Keynesian ideas to enable readers to apply them to policy questions. Readers should look here for an introduction to Keynesian thought and for its application to global policy questions, not for details of the theory or its development. Only simple graphs are used to explain Keynesian economics. If you can deal with the standard picture of supply and demand (as illustrated in figure 4.1), you have enough background to understand the essence of Keynesian economics. And we argue that the world would be better if more people understood and made use of Keynesian economics. Of course, the graphs presented in this book have many implications, and economists have been expounding and debating them for many years.

We emphasize that this book is only an introduction to Keynesian economics. It is not possible to describe the workings of the complex national and world economies fully in so small a book. You would not engage a writing coach who had mastered only an introduction to the English language, and you will not be an expert on economics after reading this book. However, a few simple graphs can lead to a major change in your understanding of the basic choices involved in making economic policies. You can become a more informed citizen.

We begin with brief surveys of a few economic analyses that were current at the time when Keynes made his primary contributions. We start by introducing an eighteenth-century view of international economic relations that runs through our exposition. The introduction provides background for our description of Keynes' early writing, his thinking at the start of the Great Depression and his innovations during the Second World War. We then survey the dominant description of the economic analysis of the domestic economy in the generation before Keynes to convey how hard it was for Keynes to depart from the existing conventions of economic analysis.

In the middle chapters, we present the familiar Keynesian analysis of a closed economy. We start with the simplest of Keynesian models and go on to more complex ones that include the monetary system. We explain why even the simplest Keynesian model is relevant to current conditions.

We then extend the domestic analysis to the international economy to show how important Keynesian ideas were to the reconstruction of the world economy after the Second World War and to the avoidance of another Great Depression. As with Keynes' more familiar analyses, we formalize his insights in a simple graph. We discuss some current problems of the world economy to show how useful simple Keynesian models can be for understanding the policy choices we now face.

We thank Robert M. Solow for helpful comments and encouragement. We thank the members of the study group on Keynesian economics at the Harvard Institute for Learning in Retirement who "road tested" the manuscript. And we thank John Covell, economics editor at the MIT Press, for his enthusiasm and help.

1
Economics before Keynes, I: Hume

Modern economics originated in eighteenth-century Britain. This should not be surprising; in the eighteenth century Britain increased its level of economic activity to a level that had been seen only in first-century Rome and seventeenth-century Holland. But although residents of these times and places may have been as well off, neither of those precursors was on its way to the Industrial Revolution. British economic thinking, distinguished as it is, is better known than other early efforts at least partly as a result of continued economic success in the English-speaking world. We introduce a few aspects of traditional economics here and in chapter 4 to describe the intellectual context in which Keynes worked.

Adam Smith, the best known of the early British economists, wrote an enduring classic that defined economics for several centuries. *The Wealth of Nations* was not entirely original; Smith drew on work done by other contemporary thinkers, who of course were not regarded as economists until after Smith wrote. Smith organized these varied thoughts into a coherent view of how parts of the economy fit together through the workings of markets, and this synthetic activity made Smith the father of modern economics. Keynes also synthesized insights of other economists of his time—insights into why the workings of markets can fail, so that resources in the economy become unemployed. Putting these new insights together created a new "Keynesian" theory. That theory has remained central to economics for almost a century.

One important eighteenth-century economic insight into international economics came from Smith's good friend David Hume. We discuss it in the first chapter of our book because international problems were important to Keynes throughout his career. Hume did not write an economic treatise comparable to Smith's *Wealth of Nations*. However, he did write several important essays about economics, one of which, "Of the Balance of Trade," provides a framework for present-day thinking about how countries fit together in the world.

In "Of the Balance of Trade," Hume considered the economy as a whole and how countries interacted. He was concerned with the dual function of specie—gold and silver coins that were used both domestically and in international trade. In the eighteenth century Britain was on a silver standard. Gold was gaining in monetary importance, and Isaac Newton, during his time as Master of the Royal Mint, tried unsuccessfully to coordinate the treatment of the two metals. If a country's exports were equal in value to the country's imports, then the importers' need for foreign currency to buy imports could be supplied by exporters who received foreign currency for their goods and services. But if a country's imports and exports were not of equal value, specie—in the form of pounds and shillings—would have to move to make up the difference. This is the problem Hume considered in "Of the Balance of Trade." Most of his discussion was narrative, describing how modern and ancient countries had gained and lost specie, but Hume preceded his narrative with a thought experiment in which he imagined the effects of assumed events. Hume stated his argument succinctly:

Suppose four fifths of all the money in Britain to be annihilated in one night, and the nation reduced to the same conditions with regard to specie as in the reigns of Harrys and Edwards; what would be the consequence? Must not the price of all labor and commodities sink in proportion, and every thing be sold as cheap as they were in those ages? What nation could then dispute with us in any foreign market or … sell manufactures at the same price which to us would afford sufficient profit? In how little time, therefore, must this bring back the money which we had lost and raise us to the level of all the neighboring nations? Where, after we have arrived, we immediately lose the advantages of the cheapness of labor and commodities, and the farther flowing in of money is stopped by our fullness and repletion.

Again, suppose that all the money in Britain were multiplied fivefold in a night, must not the contrary effect follow? … Now 'tis evident that the same causes which would correct these exorbitant inequalities, were they to happen miraculously, must prevent their happening in the common course of nature and must for ever in all neighboring nations preserve money nearly proportioned to the art and industry of each nation.

That passage introduced what economists call a model—an abstract representation of relevant aspects of reality.

How can we recognize a model? How can we evaluate a model? This is a topic we will discuss throughout the book. We introduce it here by considering model airplanes. A model airplane is also a model of an airplane. It clearly is not an airplane that one would fly in; rather, it is a small-scale representation of recognizable parts of a real airplane. A model airplane typically has a fuselage or body like one that would hold people or cargo in a real airplane, wings that would supply lift for the fuselage of a real airplane, and a tail that would stabilize the flight of a real airplane.

Regarding a model airplane as a model of an airplane, we could make use of it in various ways. We could use it to help us understand how big the wings have to be to lift the fuselage, and how to shape the wings and the fuselage so they will fit together. We could think about the placement of the tail to enhance stability and look pleasing. We could think about changing the shape of the fuselage to carry more people or to make them more comfortable. Children's models are simple, whereas airplane engineers use more complex models to design actual airplanes. Hume employed a simple model to advance his readers' understanding of international economic relations.

Hume's first thought experiment had to do with the price and the quantity of Britain's exports. When the costs of British producers were reduced to one-fifth their usual level, the quantity of exports increased. As British prices fell, imports—denominated in foreign currencies—became correspondingly more expensive. If exports rose and imports fell, how would foreigners pay for their imports (that is, British exports)? If there had been equal exchange before, then imports would have been paid for by exports. If foreigners' imports (Britain's exports) rose and their exports to Britain fell, the foreigners would have to pay for their imports in some other way. In Hume's eighteenth-century world, that meant sending specie—gold and silver coins—to Britain. As Hume noted, that would bring back to Britain the money it had lost, and would raise prices back to their initial level.

Just as a model airplane illustrates the relationship among a fuselage, wings, and a tail, Hume's model illustrates the relationship among international trade, money, and prices. Since Hume was interested primarily in the first two, his model focused on them. Hume assumed a simple relation between money and prices. His straightforward model of price determination—less money means lower prices—was popular in his time and for many years later. It became known as the Quantity Theory of Money.

Hume's second example has to do with the connection between international reserves and domestic money. If a country suffers a decline in its exports, its exports will no longer pay for its imports. It will then use specie to pay for its imports, and specie will flow out of the country. Since a domestic money supply consists largely of coins, this international transaction will decrease the domestic money stock. Since there will be less money, people will not have enough cash to pay for all the goods and services being produced at the old prices. Prices will have to fall to adjust to the lower monetary stock. Even though the exchange rate with other countries, set by the amount of gold and silver in their specie, will not have changed, what economists call the *real exchange rate* will have changed.

It is important to understand the concept of the real exchange rate. In Hume's description, the prices of domestic goods are lower relative to foreign goods than they were before, not because the exchange rate changed, but rather because prices changed. The real exchange rate is the exchange rate after allowing for any differences in prices, and it can change for either of two reasons. The nominal exchange rate can vary, or domestic prices can vary relative to foreign prices. (We refer to the nominal exchange rate throughout when we need to distinguish it from the real exchange rate.) When prices fall, as Hume explained, exports are cheaper to potential foreign buyers and imports are more expensive to potential domestic consumers. Exports rise; imports fall. The balance between exports and imports can be regained and the outward flow of specie halted. This simple process—in which a decrease in exports leads to an outflow of specie, a fall in prices, and so to a recovery in exports and a decrease in imports—is known as the *price-specie-flow model*.

We have now seen how to recognize models, illustrated by the Quantity Theory of Money and the price-specie-flow model. We also can see one way to evaluate these models, to ask if they are good or bad models. A good model provides a way for people interested in trade and prices—let us call them economists—think about problems. If economists continue to find these models useful over time, they regard these models as good ones. They remain models, not reality, and they may have to be modified as the world changes, but their insights may remain relevant nonetheless. In later chapters we will discuss how the Quantity Theory of Money and the price-specie-flow model were used two centuries later and how Keynes modified them to create a new model of modern economies.

The price-specie-flow model provided the basis for economic policies and discussions that stimulated Keynes to create different models between the two world wars. To understand how changes in the world between 1750 and 1930 affected the operation of the model, we need to consider some of the background aspects of the price-specie-flow model. We start with the relation between specie and money, progress to the relation between money and prices, then consider the relation between domestic and foreign events.

Hume assumed that specie made up most of Britain's supply of money. The amount of specie then determined the amount of money. Banks were in their infancy in 1750, and Hume did not consider their effects on the money supply important. True, the Bank of England and a handful of London goldsmith banks already existed, but their effects on the total economy were still small. Hume's assumption was a reasonable simplification of the world he knew.

As national economies grew in the nineteenth century, trade between them also grew. Gold supplanted silver as the primary way to transfer money internationally, and Europe and America moved onto what we now know as the gold standard. They then committed to buy and sell their currencies for gold at the fixed price. This was the system that was in place when Keynes began to write.

Commercial banks grew in the nineteenth century, and central banks began to exert their influence through the banking system. Banks held deposits that their customers could draw against. They held specie as reserves, but after they discovered that not all depositors came in at once they began to hold less specie for every pound or shilling of deposit. This fractional-reserve banking allowed the supply of money to grow faster than the supply of specie. When a lot of depositors came in at once, as in a banking panic, the banks were in trouble if they did not have enough reserves to pay everyone. Central banks increasingly stepped in to save banks in distress and to reduce the impact of banking panics on economic activity.

As was explained earlier, Hume assumed that the overall price level was determined by the amount of money in what became known as the Quantity Theory of Money. As he asked in his essay, "Must not the price of all labor and commodities sink in proportion" [if the money supply decreases]? Money consequently was a "veil" over the "real" economy; the change in the overall price level did not have any effects on the price of one good in terms of another good, that is, on relative prices. In modern economies, this may be true in the long run but it is far from accurate in the short run. Nineteenth-century economists were not able to explain the mechanism by which the quantity of money affected prices. Following Hume, they simply assumed that less money led to lower prices.

This was fine for a pre-industrial economy, even an advanced one such as eighteenth-century Britain. But the Industrial Revolution started late in that century and continued into the next. Industrial firms started small, but the growth of railroads and steamships led to the growth of large firms during the nineteenth century and the early twentieth century. The growth of these firms created problems for the Quantity Theory of Money. Large companies often set out lists of prices that they were reluctant to change. They also employed many hundreds of workers, who resisted wage cuts with various kinds of collective actions.

Economists speak of these new industrial price and wage behaviors as *sticky prices*. A decrease in the supply of money will not lower all prices at the same rate if some of them are sticky prices. In particular, it may lower product prices while wages remain resistant to wage cuts. Hume lived in an agricultural society, whereas we live in an industrial one or even a post-industrial one. Agricultural prices and wages move up and down in response to changes in the supply of and the demand for workers, crops, and animals. But industrial prices move upward far more easily than they move downward, and it is very hard to reduce wages in industrial economies.

The change to sticky prices led to an asymmetric response to a rise and a decrease in exports in Hume's price-specie-flow model for the same reasons the Quantity Theory of Money ran into problems. The growth of large firms in the late nineteenth century led to large concentrations of workers in factories and cities. Industrial workers resisted wage cuts, although they cheerfully accepted wage increases. This asymmetry was true before unions were strong, and it continues to be true even now that the strength of unions has declined. It was noted by Keynes during the Great Depression, and economists and policy makers alike dealt with its consequences at that time. Keynes worked hard to incorporate this fact of modern life into his overall view of the economy.

The price-specie-flow model can be expanded easily to take account of this change. When exports decrease relative to imports in this more modern version, employment falls. The decline in the money stock leads—by mechanisms we will detail later—to a reduction in the quantity of work instead of a reduction in the pay for work. Unemployment instead of deflation is the response to external imbalance. Economists today refer to this asymmetry as Keynesian because Keynes emphasized it in *The General Theory* but Keynes described it as an empirical fact well before he wrote that book. When Keynes wrote *A Treatise on Money*, published in 1930, he still assumed full employment and appealed to the original form of the price-specie flow mechanism, revealing how hard it was to incorporate uncomfortable empirical facts into a theoretical account.

Recall Hume's question "Must not the price of all labor and commodities sink in proportion?" Economic progress since Hume's time requires us to modify this question in several ways. The supply of money is dependent partly on banks, rather than the supply of specie. When banks lose reserves, they may raise their interest rates in order to convince depositors to maintain their deposits. Central banks may raise interest rates in an attempt to regain specie if they think that will help commercial banks. And wages and prices may not fall if the interest rate rises or even if the quantity of money falls.

This brings us back to the real exchange rate—that is, the nominal exchange rate times the ratio of prices. Hume assumed that the nominal exchange rate could not change, and that all adjustments in the real exchange rate had to be made by price changes. But if prices are sticky, we have to think about the alternative: changing the nominal exchange rate, either by devaluation or appreciation of the currency. Discussion in 1930 was firmly in the tradition of Hume, but it changed soon thereafter in the crisis of the Great Depression. Countries departed from the gold standard under pressure and began to depreciate their currencies. Since then we have lived in a world in which currencies are able to devalue or appreciate against other currencies. Europe however has returned to the framework introduced by Hume in which internal price deflations become important. Why? Prices have not returned to their pre-industrial behavior, but the discipline of the gold standard—abandoned in the Great Depression—has returned in the Eurozone.

The beginning of the price-specie-flow process can be described as an *external imbalance*, since it is the result of a change of exports without a corresponding change in imports. This process leads to an outcome that can be described as an *internal imbalance*, since the reduction of the money stock led to a deflation—that is, to a decrease in prices. The connection between external and internal imbalances is one of the central features of Keynesian thought. Some economists today are concerned primarily with the need for internal balance within isolated economies; others are concerned mainly with the need to balance international trade, considering only external balance. Keynes spent the interwar years trying to understand these linkages in the midst of the Great Depression. He did not understand them fully in 1930, but he had a clear grasp of them a decade later. However, before we get to discussions in 1930, we need to examine Keynes' thoughts at the conclusion of the First World War.

2

Keynes at Versailles

Keynes was in charge of the international aspects of Britain's economic policy by the end of the First World War, even though he was then only in his mid thirties. He was sent to Paris after the war as the chief Treasury representative of the British delegation at the negotiations that led to the Treaty of Versailles, but at the end of June 1919 he resigned in fury at what was happening in these negotiations. Returning to Britain, he slipped away to a country house that was the rural retreat of artistic friends from the Bloomsbury group and quickly wrote *The Economic Consequences of the Peace* to protest what had happened at Versailles. Keynes leapt to international fame when that book was published.

The Economic Consequences of the Peace can be read in two ways. It is a marvelous polemic, written briskly in a style that still communicates well after almost a century. In addition, it reveals the view of the world economy that occupied Keynes' thoughts from then until his untimely death in 1946, including an understanding of how a well-functioning international economy is meant to work, what can go wrong, and the policies needed to rectify the failings. It also shows how his insights were translated into economic theories.

The polemical nature of *The Economic Consequences of the Peace* shines most brightly in Keynes' description of the major architects of the Treaty of Versailles. He described how Georges Clemenceau bamboozled Woodrow Wilson into a Carthaginian Peace. The reference is to the Romans' actions after defeating Carthage over 2,000 years ago. They forced Carthage to pay a continuing tribute to Rome (anticipating the reparations imposed on Germany at Versailles), to demilitarize, and not to make war without Rome's permission. When that was not enough to cow the Carthaginians, Rome burned Carthage to the ground and enslaved the population after another Punic War. An equally cruel description of David Lloyd George came later in *The Economic Consequences of the Peace*:

Keynes accused him of greatly increasing the size of German reparations to win reelection in 1918.

Keynes prefaced his analysis of the Versailles negotiations and the treaty that resulted with a description of economic conditions before the Great War in order to set up a contrast with the dismal postwar conditions he described later. He opened his discussion with a paragraph that has been quoted widely ever since:

> The inhabitant of London could order by telephone, sipping his morning tea in bed, the various products of the whole earth, in such quantity as he might see fit, and reasonably expect their early delivery upon his doorstep; he could at the same moment and by the same means adventure his wealth in the natural resources and new enterprises of any quarter of the world, and share, without exertion or even trouble, in their prospective fruits and advantages; or he could decide to couple the security of his fortunes with the good faith of the townspeople of any substantial municipality in any continent that fancy or information might recommend. He could secure forthwith, if he wished it, cheap and comfortable means of transit to any country or climate without passport or other formality, could dispatch his servant to the neighbouring office of a bank for such supply of the precious metals as might seem convenient, and could then proceed abroad to foreign quarters, without knowledge of their religion, language, or customs, bearing coined wealth upon his person, and would consider himself greatly aggrieved and much surprised at the least interference. But, most important of all, he regarded this state of affairs as normal, certain, and permanent, except in the direction of further improvement, and any deviation from it as aberrant, scandalous, and avoidable.

In that paean to prewar prosperity, Keynes revealed his interest in the long-run process of economic growth. Rome was not built in a day, nor was what we now call Late Victorian Prosperity. Britain had a century of industrial leadership that made it the "workshop of the world" by the middle of the nineteenth century, and the exhibition that marked its status was housed in a building (Crystal Palace) that was as much a result of new technologies as the exhibits it contained. Britain had exported its technology and its products around the world and in the process had emerged as the world's financial center. When other countries could not pay for railroads or even cotton goods on their own, the British were happy to lend them money. By the beginning of the twentieth century, British consumers enjoyed themselves, as Keynes described, both as a result of sales of new goods and as a result of earnings provided by the bonds they had bought from abroad.

In a remarkable few pages in *The Economic Consequences of the Peace*, Keynes set out to explain how this process of growth had worked for Europe as a whole. He first showed that technological development and rapid population growth had made it possible for the output of the

European economy to grow at an unprecedented rate. In addition, Keynes observed that wages remained low and profits were high:

[T]he inequality of the distribution of wealth which made possible those vast accumulations of fixed wealth and of capital improvements which distinguished that age from all others.

This was in line with Adam Smith's observation that poor people do not save and accumulate resources. It is the rich who save, and who accumulate the capital that makes economic growth possible. Furthermore,

There grew round the non-consumption of the cake ... instincts of puritanism. ... And so the cake increased [by means of capital accumulation]; but to what end was not contemplated. ... Individuals [were inclined] not so much to abstain as to defer [consumption].

This was a world in which high profits would lead to rapid growth unencumbered by uncertainty and any shortage of demand. Keynes believed that this growth process was international, supported by the international trading system. Although Keynes was writing about Germany and its relations with the rest of Europe, it is clear that he thought that something similar was happening in the relations among Britain, its empire, and the Americas. This growth process required global trade and investment:

On the prosperity and enterprise of Germany, the prosperity of the rest of the Continent mainly depended. The increasing pace of Germany gave her neighbors an outlet for their products, in exchange for which the enterprise of the German merchant supplied them with their chief requirements at a low price. ... Germany not only furnished these countries with trade, but, in the case of some of them, supplied a great part of the capital needed for their own development.

The accumulative habits of Europe before the war were the necessary condition [for this growth process]: ... of the surplus capital goods accumulated by Europe a substantial part was exported abroad, where its investment made possible the development of the new resources of food materials and transport, and enabled the Old World to stake out a claim on in the natural wealth and virgin potentialities of the New.

Keynes argued that Germany was the key to European prosperity because it exported manufactures to other European countries, and that Europe as a whole was important to world prosperity because it exported manufactures to Asia, the British Empire, and the Americas in return for raw materials and food. In each case, trade improved prosperity by allowing countries to exploit their comparative advantages. Keynes asserted that the resulting trade benefited all countries and assumed that the gains from trade were invested wisely.

This system clearly depended on foreign lending, as Keynes said. Like Britain, Germany exported products even to countries that could not pay for them with exports. It lent other countries money to invest in German products, as Britain had done before, to expand its markets. This was a world system in the sense that it extended throughout Europe and the United States, although it only penetrated isolated countries outside this industrial center. Production was needed for this prosperity, as was the willingness of investors in Britain and Germany to forgo consumption from their earnings to invest in the prospects that other countries would grow in response to their contacts with the industrial leaders. We call the policies of Britain and Germany in that period *export-led growth*.

Early in his career, Keynes set out a theory of economic growth that was worked out formally after the Second World War. Growth starts when technical progress in one country leads to an expansion of productive capacity, but living standards do not increase as soon or as fast as production. New business firms have to search abroad for additional markets, giving rise to export-led growth. Keynes described this in England and Germany; we have seen it more recently in Japan and China. Keynes is more relevant today than many current growth theories because he recognized the international aspects of economic growth.

To summarize: Keynes saw prosperity before the World War as the result of the working of a world economic system, although he is celebrated today primarily for his contributions to the analysis of a *closed economy* (that is, an economy without foreign trade or investments). Clearly, Keynes knew that domestic prosperity was critically determined by external conditions. As he emphasized throughout *The Economic Consequences of the Peace*, domestic prosperity cannot be attained without external prosperity. He later struggled to extend this view in 1930 in front of the Macmillan Committee and again in the 1940s before and during the Bretton Woods Conference (the 1944 conference that resulted in the establishment of the International Monetary Fund). Clarifying this view was the primary aim of his professional career.

This is not appreciated properly today. Keynes turned to Britain's domestic problems in the 1930s as part of his search to understand world economic problems. *The General Theory of Employment, Interest and Money* (1936) summarized this basic part of Keynesian thought. It is a great book, and most people think of Keynes as simply the author of this one book. They think that Keynes has little or no relevance to current economic problems as countries seek prosperity in an open world economy. We argue that this is a restricted view of Keynes that focuses on only one part of his career and ignores the breadth of his economic vision.

At the end of chapter 2 of *The Economic Consequences of the Peace*, Keynes says that he has drawn a picture of the world economy before the First World War not only to show the reasons for its success but also to show how vulnerable it was. He says that he

selected for emphasis the three or four greatest factors of instability—the instability of an excessive population dependent for its livelihood on a complicated and artificial organisation, the psychological instability of the labouring and the capitalist classes, and the instability of Europe's claim, coupled with her dependence, on the food supplies of the New World.

The rest of Keynes' career was devoted to identifying reasons for such vulnerability, and to devising policies that would stop this vulnerability from derailing the global growth process.

We need to stop a minute to consider the role of foreign lending and foreign bonds in creating such vulnerability. A bond is the record of a loan that one person, company, or country makes to another. It often lasts for several years and is part of the long-run process of economic growth. Export-led growth depends on the existence of such bonds. Economic growth takes a long time, and long-term bonds can be useful in the process. British and German holdings of foreign bonds were useful to Britain and Germany as well as to the developing countries who issued these bonds. The sale of bonds enabled these developing countries to finance the construction of railways and new cities. They purchased the manufactures of the advanced countries, and this purchase made possible the export-led growth of the advanced countries. Keynes recalled that Germany exported capital to other European countries to enable them to buy German exports before the First World War. Any reader today will recognize this pattern a century later as a prominent feature of the Eurozone during the first decade of the twenty-first century, when borrowing in southern Europe made a rapid expansion of German exports possible. It is uncanny that this pattern has reasserted itself throughout the twentieth century and the early twenty-first century, both after the world wars and at other times. As we will see, current problems echo the problems Keynes anticipated in this process of export-led growth.

The international system described above was durable as long as the expectations implicit in any bond were realized. The developing countries needed to acquire enough foreign exchange to service their bonds, and the mature economies needed to provide a stable market for foreign bonds. As we explain more thoroughly in chapter 6, people and companies choose between holding bonds and holding cash in response to the current interest rate and their expectations about future interest rates. And, as we explain in chapter 10, expectations about the return on foreign bonds can create disorder in anticipation.

Expectations played an important part in the well-known models of the closed economy that Keynes set out in *The General Theory of Employment, Interest and Money* in the 1930s. But they also played an important part in the earlier account of Victorian prosperity that Keynes set out in *The Economic Consequences of the Peace*. British investors held bonds from developing countries because they firmly expected those bonds to hold their value and be serviced reliably. (Those expectations were fulfilled in most years, although they occasionally failed miserably during financial crises.) Keynes never formulated a theory of expectations; instead he asserted they were determined by "animal spirits" that remained stable "when the ocean is flat" but were subject to panics during storms.

In the remainder of *The Economics Consequences of the Peace* Keynes identified the reparations imposed on Germany at Versailles as leading to the instability that, he argued, made the process of economic growth vulnerable. He saw reparations as economically irrational and politically unwise. He argued that reparations functioned like German debts; they would reverse the position of Germany in Europe. Germany would go from being a cheerful creditor of other nations to a reluctant and recalcitrant borrower. The preceding period of prosperity would be thrown into confusion by this reversal of economic relations between European countries.

Let us be clear about the economics of reparations in order to understand their effect on interwar prosperity. Germany had been running an export surplus as part of its export-led growth before the war. Reparations compelled Germany to run an export surplus after the war to pay reparations. How had Germany's position changed? It had gone from a creditor to a debtor. Reparations enforced upon Germany a huge capital loss. Instead of being a rich country that could choose whether to export its products, Germany was to become a poor country that was forced to export its products.

France and England wanted reparations because they had been impoverished by the First World War. They had acquired huge war debts to the United States in order to fight the war. Since the United States refused to cancel those debts, France and England would have to restrain the consumption of their citizens. They wanted Germany to restrain the consumption of its citizens instead. In other words, they wanted to transfer their losses to Germany. Germany then would have to force saving, that is, restrain German consumption. That would degrade the quality of life in Germany, as Keynes described vividly:

The policy of reducing Germany to servitude for a generation, of degrading the lives of millions of human beings, and of depriving a whole nation of happiness should be abhorrent and detestable—abhorrent and detestable, even if it were possible, even if it enriched ourselves, even if [it] did not sow the decay of the whole civilised life of Europe.

This clear statement of the problem shows that Keynes had conceptualized one of the difficult problems of international economic relations— something that later became known as the *transfer problem*. This problem anticipates difficulties in today's world that have had their origins in the architecture of the European Monetary System and in the export-led growth strategy of Japan and China. Today's problems did not arise from a military conquest, but that does not mean that the solution of the transfer problem is any easier today than it was in the 1920s.

Keynes would continue to work on this problem for the next quarter of a century. He would come to see that, even if Germany was to make forced savings, and reduce its expenditures relative to its production, and try to export more than it imported, that would not be enough. In order for the exports to be demanded by other countries, residents of those countries would have to increase their expenditure relative to their production. Thus, Keynes would come to see that it was not enough for Germany to spend less and export more; other countries would have to consume more to buy the German exports. If they did not do so, a global recession would result from this attempt to make Germany pay reparations. And Keynes would see that the Allies were unlikely to do this in a world in which Germany was cutting its expenditures. Keynes would also come to understand difficulties created by the gold standard. On the gold standard, it would be hard for the repaying country, Germany, to make its goods cheap enough for others to wish to buy them in a world in because it could not devalue its currency as a way of cheapening its goods abroad. In 1919 Keynes did not yet understand these things fully.

Nevertheless, even in 1919 Keynes could see that the benefits of capital flows were not certain. According to Keynes' reminiscence in 1919, educated Britons and their counterparts in other countries saw worldwide markets as the normal state of affairs. Businessmen, bankers, and their professional offspring moved easily among cities from Berlin to New York. The gold standard—with its corollary that citizens in one country could freely lend to those in other countries—symbolized the mentality and patterns of conduct of these intellectual and economic elites. But Keynes had come to see the economic system that lay between these patterns of conduct as vulnerable.

Keynes predicted continued hostility and opposition to the Treaty of Versailles and to reparations. He did not foresee any cooperative movements by any of the previous combatants:

All these influences ... favour a continuation of the present conditions instead of a recovery from them. An inefficient, unemployed, disorganized Europe faces us, torn by internal strife and international hate, fighting, starving, pillaging, and lying. What warrant is there for a picture of less somber colors?

The Economic Consequences of the Peace shows that Keynes thought about international economic relations and that he was concerned with the long run as well as the short run. His international concerns led him to an understanding of the role that international trade played in making rapid growth possible, and to an understanding that such trade arises when one region incurs debts to be able to purchase increased exports from another region. He also understood the problems that arise when debts must be repaid, and how debts could retard the process of long-run growth. But he did not yet have any means of analyzing the behavior of an economy suffering from the need to make such a transfer. He would deal with similar problems at the end of the Second World War.

In the final chapter of *The Economic Consequences of the Peace*, Keynes described ways to alleviate the pain he was certain would result from the Treaty of Versailles. One possibility was an international loan from the United States. But, Keynes admitted,

There is no guarantee that Europe will put financial assistance to proper use, or that she will not squander it and be in just as bad case two or three years hence as she is in now. ... If I had influence at the United States Treasury, I would not lend a penny to a single one of the present Governments of Europe. They are not to be trusted with resources which they would devote to the furtherance of policies in repugnance to ... the United States.

The United States did extend a large loan to Germany five years later, and it was squandered as Keynes predicted. The first of two huge loans allowed Germany to end its hyperinflation in 1924 by allowing Germany to pay reparations without restricting German consumption. It would have been better for the United States to have forgiven war debts and let the Allies reduce reparations, but that would have required a degree of international cooperation that could not be found so soon after the Versailles peace conference.

Only six years later, the United States tried to stem growing economic troubles in Germany with another huge loan that, unhappily, could not repeat even the limited success of the earlier loan. Keynes recognized that attitudes and expectations would have to be more optimistic and cooperative than those that had prevailed at Versailles in order for specific actions to be effective.

Keynes condemned reparations as economically irrational and politically unwise. He argued that the Treaty of Versailles was not sensible, and that it was against the best interests of the victorious powers to cripple Germany economically insofar as much of Europe's pre-1914 welfare had depended on German economic growth. Moreover, Keynes envisaged difficulties in transferring real resources across borders, in view of uncertainty about how the postwar international capital market would work. His overall view was that reparations were vindictive and ultimately unworkable; they would lead to continued conflict, not to peace. *The Economic Consequences of the Peace* sold well and established Keynes as a global public intellectual. It also set the agenda for his subsequent research.

Keynes had set out a vision of how the Europe economy and the global economy had functioned well during the British Century—a remarkable period of economic expansion sometime referred to as the Second Industrial Revolution. He understood the symbiotic nature of national economies and would use that framework in his future research. He mapped out the challenge of making such a growth miracle happen again. He began this task after Versailles and continued it in his appearance before the Macmillan Committee in 1930, with the writing of *The General Theory of Employment, Interest and Money*, and with his work at the Bretton Woods Conference.

The analysis in *Economic Consequences of the Peace* continues to be relevant today. Keynes noted that global growth was dependent on German capital exports before the First World War, and that this global growth process would be undermined by the imposition of reparations payments on Germany. As we discuss in chapter 9, a similar dramatic shift recently took place in Europe.

3

Keynes and the Macmillan Committee

Economic conditions in the 1920s were even more depressing than Keynes had predicted in *The Economic Consequences of the Peace*. The first half of the decade was replete with hyperinflations and bank crises all across Europe. Germany resisted paying reparations—the "debt" it had inherited from the war and the Treaty of Versailles. France invaded Germany's coal and steel areas to force the Germans to pay up. Germany responded by inflating its currency to reduce its debt, resulting in a famous hyperinflation. At the same time, Britain was deflating its currency in order to return to the gold standard at the old rate. The internal strife generated by Britain's deflation culminated in a general strike as the government strove to reduce wages.

This turbulent period was brought to an end by a huge loan from the United States to Germany in 1924 that enabled the Germans to end their hyperinflation and regain the appearance of normality. The rest of the decade appeared likely to be prosperous for each country by itself, but the poisonous effects of international obligations suggested that this economic edifice was built on sand. As Keynes had predicted, the American loan didn't eliminate the international flows of capital which were required by the repayment of war loans and by reparations, and it didn't eliminate the Germans' resentment of reparations—the national debt they had incurred at Versailles.

At the end of the 1920s, Germany and then the United States went into recession. The causes of these recessions are neither clear nor important; they both came from imbalances that led to unsustainable booms in municipal spending in Germany and stock-market prices in the United States. Recession in the two main industrial countries caused distress throughout Europe and the wider world.

Britain's economic position at the end of the 1920s was particularly dire. The country had returned to the gold standard at an uncompetitive exchange rate in 1925, and its economy had been radically weakened by the war. Its holdings of overseas assets had been significantly reduced to pay for the war, curtailing income from abroad. Much of the country's productive capital hadn't been replaced or modernized since before the war, and its capacity to export had contracted during the hostilities, never to be rebuilt. In these circumstances, Britain needed lower costs to make the country once again internationally competitive. Only then could it regain its position as a country with good growth prospects in which firms would invest and people had jobs and felt confident enough to spend freely. But the required improvement in competitiveness failed to materialize, and devaluation had been ruled out during the war.

At the same time, the persistence of the British Empire and the alliance of Canada, Australia, and New Zealand as members of the new British Commonwealth meant that London was still the center of the financial world. By contrast, Germany was preoccupied with internal conflicts and was much more interested in maintaining its opposition to the former allies than in cooperating with them. The Americans retreated into isolation. There was no other power that could fulfill a leadership role.

The combination of a difficult economic position and a sense of global responsibility created particular difficulties for British politics. A new Labour government came to power in the election of May 1929. By October, policy making was overwhelmed by the Wall Street crash. Soon afterward, the prime minister did what British governments often do at a time of difficulty: He created a Committee of Enquiry. It became known as the Macmillan Committee after its chairman, a Scottish judge. The Macmillan Committee wasn't required to advise on any particular economic policy question, but was charged with carrying out a wide-ranging investigation of the options facing Britain and the rest of the world.

Keynes was by far the most eminent member of the Macmillan Committee, and it is remembered today only for what he said there. He had cast himself out from the center of imperial power in London by publishing *The Economic Consequences of the Peace*. He had given up the opportunity of rising to the top of the British civil service, something that was clearly within his grasp. But he was one of the cleverest people in the country, had a mesmerizing personality, and was a ruthless operator. With numerous publications, he had contrived to remain at the center of British commentaries on politics, and he had achieved vast influence on economic policy, even if from the outside.

The committee met more than a hundred times during 1930. Evidence was taken on 49 days, and a report was published in June of 1931.

Keynes was central to what happened, both in examining witnesses and in shaping the report. He was asked to advance the members' thinking by presenting his ideas for five days in the early stages of the committee's work and for three days when the committee was beginning to draft its report. Thus Keynes was granted an extraordinary opportunity to present his own views and to shape the committee's work.

Keynes' presentations completely captivated the committee. The minutes of the relevant meetings occupy nearly 300 pages in Keynes' *Collected Works*. Keynes maintained the structure of his argument over a five-day set of presentations. He was extraordinarily careful in presenting each detail of his argument and made extended detours to answer specific questions from the members of the committee who formed his audience. He moved easily between general principles and particular examples, showing a subtle command of language and a sense of which ideas he should restated to ensure that those present fully understood what he said. Lord Macmillan, who was ignorant about finance but who was open-minded and sympathetic, summarized the feelings of the committee. At the close of the fourth day of Keynes' presentations in February, Macmillan told him that members of the committee "hardly notice the lapse of time when you are speaking."

Keynes' preparation for the Macmillan Committee went back ten years to *The Economic Consequences of the Peace*. It was widely known that Keynes had been working on a restatement of monetary theory for the previous five years, bringing Alfred Marshall's tradition up to date, and that the resulting *Treatise on Money* was in the process of publication as the committee convened for its meetings. The *Treatise on Money* was written in the late 1920s, when the world was prosperous. It therefore extended Marshall's tradition with the Quantity Theory of Money intact. Prices were flexible, and they could move to equilibrate all markets. Since Britain's primary problem in 1930 was unemployment, however, Keynes' work didn't help him as much as he hoped. In fact, the Macmillan Committee is of interest to us because Keynes' presentations to it didn't add up to a coherent view. Rather, they show Keynes thinking on his feet at a time when his ideas were in flux.

Keynes was aware that his testimony didn't add up, and his inability to attract any of the other members of the committee to his views set the stage for the work he was to carry out for the next fifteen years. It led him to focus on two great questions for these final years of his life: How can extensive and continuing unemployment be alleviated? How can countries at different levels of income and in different states of economic development interact with each other in economic harmony? His answers to these questions enabled Keynes to turn the vision of his age he had expounded in *The Economic Consequences of the Peace* into a system for managing the world economy.

Keynes began his presentations to the Macmillan Committee with a discussion of the gold standard:

> I have decided that probably the best way will be to begin rather in the middle and then work forwards and backwards, starting from the things that are probably relatively familiar and keeping till the last some of the things which I hold of great importance, but which are likely to be less familiar. I think it will be useful if, first of all, we go through the more or less orthodox theory of how Bank rate works, the classical theory of Bank rate as it has existed in this country for the last 50 years.
>
> So long as we are on the gold standard, the fundamental principle of our currency management has to be that the differences between our international receipts and payments which we have to meet or receive in gold shall never be very large. We cannot afford to lose large quantities of gold, or at any rate to lose them continuously. So ... the primary task of currency management is to keep an approximate equality between our international receipts and payments. This balance is made up of two parts.

Keynes took his cue from the practice of the Bank of England over the previous century, possibly as described in Walter Bagehot's *Lombard Street*, a book published about 50 years earlier. Bagehot had argued that in times of financial crisis banks should lend freely to businesses at interest rates high enough that only those in need would borrow. Keynes expanded Hume's model of the balance of payments by introducing the interest rate into the picture, although the price-specie-flow mechanism remained central to his message.

The first component of the expanded gold-standard mechanism—a short-term component—worked as follows. If a country was exporting less than it imported, then it would be the task of its monetary authority (for example, the Bank of England) to raise the interest rate—known in Britain as "Bank rate"—in order to attract funds from abroad, and thereby to cover the cost of imports. This action could cushion the deficit that a country was experiencing, ensuring that it attracted enough gold to pay for its imports. The Bank of England was at the center of this international financial system, and it had a lot of experience with adjusting Bank rate in this way. Keynes described how well the Bank of England was able to operate this short-term cushioning of the effects of a deficit.

Hume's price-specie-flow model had been a theoretical exercise; there was no consideration of the way the money supply would rise or fall dramatically. Keynes started from a real phenomenon: the loss of foreign exchange reserves due to a decrease in *net exports*, that is, a decrease in exports or an increase in imports. The Bank of England existed when Hume wrote, but it was engaged more in financing England's wars than in preserving England's gold reserves. In the course of the nineteenth century, the Bank of England became far more active in maintaining the country's reserves (that is, its external balance). As Keynes said, the Bank adopted the so-called Palmer Rule, raising the interest rate when a decrease in net exports led to a reduction of gold reserves.

But, Keynes claimed, such short-term cushioning couldn't solve the underlying external difficulty facing an economy like that of Britain. He described a longer-term component of the gold-standard mechanism that required holding the interest rate at a high level long enough to cause a decrease in investment and induce a decrease in the overall demand for domestic goods. This, in turn, would lead to in an increase in unemployment that would cause wages to fall. Unemployment had to remain high for a sufficiently long period, and wages had to fall by a sufficiently large amount, for the economy to become competitive again. The economy would then be able to gain export markets again, and it would export enough to pay for its imports. It would no longer need high interest rates to attract funds from abroad. Keynes said there is no other way for Bank rate to bring down prices, except by increasing unemployment. That, he concluded, "is the beginning and end of traditional sound finance in this country."

The longer-term component of the adjustment mechanism was first proposed by Hume in the price-specie-flow mechanism described earlier. But the short-term component, which entailed use of Bank rate, was missing from Hume's account because Hume subscribed to what is now called the Quantity Theory of Money. On that theory, expenditures are determined directly by the quantity of money. If gold flows out of a country because the country isn't exporting enough, its residents will have less money and will spend less; that will set in motion the longer-term component of Keynes' mechanism, and prices will fall.

By inserting an intermediate step that depends on the interest rate, Keynes was rejecting the Quantity Theory of Money. That may not sound like a radical innovation to a modern audience, but it was new in 1930. Hume used the Quantity Theory of Money to argue that the level of prices in an economy was determined by the quantity of money in existence. That idea had become a central idea in the teaching of economics, for it was a necessary part of any attempt to connect monetary phenomena (prices) with real phenomena (how many actual goods and services are bought and sold in an economy) in the absence of what we now call Keynesian macroeconomics. Ever since Keynes had begun lecturing at the University of Cambridge (in 1909, the year Marshall retired), he had passed on the Marshallian tradition to generations of Cambridge students. By the 1920s, he had become the leading authority on Hume, Marshall, the Quantity Theory, and the gold standard in Cambridge and worldwide.

Yet now he separated the workings of the gold-standard mechanism into two components: a short-term effect on capital inflows, operating as a result of a rise in Bank rate, and a longer-term effect, operating through an improvement in competitiveness that was caused by the unemployment that was caused by the increase in Bank rate. This seems rather trite to us; it is something that we all now understand. But it was a dramatic change of view for his audience in 1930.

Keynes didn't yet completely understand an important part of his own argument, and the governor of the Bank of England, Montagu Norman, understood almost nothing that Keynes said. Governor Norman was blinded by the Quantity Theory of Money to a century of history of the Bank of England. This became evident later in the proceedings of the Macmillan Committee when Norman was called upon to give evidence. Asked to describe his view of the workings of the gold standard, Norman categorically refused to accept Keynes' analysis. He thought the Bank of England's responsibilities extended only to the short-term component of the gold-standard mechanism, that of ensuring sufficient capital inflow at times of inadequate exports to avoid the country losing gold. The idea that the Bank of England actually caused the unemployment problems that Keynes attributed to the workings of the gold standard was beyond him. Wage adjustment was, he said, a matter for industry, and for its workers: "I have never been able to see myself why for the last few years it should have been impossible for industry, starting from within, to have readjusted its own position."

The minutes of the Macmillan Committee show that Keynes made Governor Norman look foolish and that the committee agreed with Keynes' view that Norman's answers were hopelessly inadequate. Indeed, Norman's evidence was so threadbare and so deliberately negative that, according to Norman's biographer, the deputy governor of the Bank of England was given the unenviable task of doctoring the evidence for the printed record.

The minutes of the committee also show that its members came to agree with Keynes that the gold-standard adjustment process had a short-run component and a longer-run component. Toward the end of his first day of presentations, Keynes sought to bring together these two components. How long will it take for adjustment to happen, he asked? That depends, he argued, on how resistant wages are to falling.

Keynes expressed doubt whether the longer-term component of the adjustment process could be made to work adequately, except when wages were growing and adjustment required only that wages grow less rapidly. That, Keynes maintained, was why the gold standard had worked satisfactorily in the late nineteenth century. Keynes denied that money wages had ever been downwardly flexible in the way that was now required:

My reading of history is that for centuries there has existed an intense social resistance to any matters of reduction in the level of money incomes. I believe that, apart from the adjustments due to cyclical fluctuations, there has never been in modern or ancient history any community that has been prepared to accept without immense struggle a reduction in the general level of money income. ... The ... deflation which followed the Napoleonic Wars, ... very much like the one we are going through now, was one which brought the country to the verge of revolution. ...

These problems of wage adjustment explained why problems emerged after Britain rejoined the gold standard in 1925. The British government decided during the First World War that prices would be reduced after the war, to allow reestablishment of the prewar value of the pound, and it tried to implement that decision by attempting to lower wages. That policy decision, Keynes thought, led to the miners' strike and then the general strike of 1926, to the collapse of the Lancashire cotton industry in the late 1920s and to widespread unemployment in Britain by 1930.

Keynes' allegation drew a sharp response from Lord Bradbury, who had chaired the committee that had recommended the return to the gold standard in 1925. A lively debate between Bradbury and Keynes ensued, joined by other members of the committee; it continued into the next day. Unlike Montagu Norman, other members of the committee agreed with Keynes on how the adjustment process was meant to work. But unlike Keynes, they believed that it could be made to work in the way that was required.

This controversy seems eerily like the one now taking place within the European Monetary Union. Greece, Ireland, Italy, Portugal, and Spain are now uncompetitive in relation to Germany. But within the monetary union, these countries are unable to devalue their exchange rate relative to Germany, just as countries were unable to do within the gold-standard system. There is now intense debate whether it will be possible to reduce wages in these countries enough to enable economic growth to resume.

Industrial workers resist wage reductions because they are located together in factories and cities. They see what is happening around them, and they fear that their wages are being cut more than prices and the salaries of other people. They don't want to bear the brunt of costly adjustments needed to make the economy work better. They argue—in the only ways open to them—that they aren't getting their share of the rewards of progress. This sense was particularly acute in the 1920s after workers had borne the brunt of trench warfare during the First World War, a war that had started far from their households and their factories. They were expecting rewards for their patriotism, not demands for more sacrifice.

Keynes didn't believe that British wages would fall rapidly or far enough to restore external balance. The gold standard couldn't work in 1930 to restore external balance. Some kind of remedy was needed. During the subsequent presentations of his evidence, Keynes outlined three remedies, just as he had discussed possible remedies to the parlous situation a decade earlier in the final chapter of *The Economic Consequences of the Peace.*

The first remedy Keynes proposed was a devaluation of the pound— that is, a departure by Britain from the gold standard. After devaluation, a British pound would buy less foreign currency, and foreigners would be able to buy more pounds with their foreign currency. That would cheapen the price of British goods in world markets when expressed in foreign currency, and the amount of British exports would rise. It would also raise the price of imports, measured in pounds, within Britain. As a result, the demand for British goods would increase as people bought British-produced goods instead of the more expensive imports. This was Hume's price-specie-flow mechanism with a decrease in the nominal exchange rate rather than a decrease in domestic prices.

Keynes, however, believed that such a route through devaluation of the currency was not a viable option for Britain, even though in 1925 he had been a fervent opponent of the return to the gold standard at an overvalued exchange rate. The Macmillan Committee's deliberations, including Keynes' presentations, show that members of the committee didn't consider at any length the alternative of abandoning the gold standard, so great was the respect for that standard. Yet the gold standard was in fact abandoned only three months after the publication of the committee's report.

Keynes surely would have pushed for a devaluation if there had been the remotest chance that it would be accepted; he didn't lack the necessary courage, and he had previously devoted several years to strenuous opposition to Britain's return to gold. But once Britain had returned to the gold standard, Keynes believed that Britain should stay the course. Anything else would reduce confidence in the City of London as a global financial center. And preserving that confidence was essential to ensuring global recovery.

Finding himself in a quandary, Keynes then produced a second possible remedy. This was a really remarkable proposal for him. He suggested that some measure of protection for British goods by means of tariffs might be desirable as a temporary remedy for the current impasse. Up to that point, Keynes had been a determined free-trader. But he now argued that protection would increase the demand for British goods, and thereby boost British employment. But although protection would cause an increase in the demand for import substitutes within Britain, it wouldn't lead to an increase in exports in the same way that would happen after a devaluation of the currency or a cut in wages. As a consequence, protection would be inefficient.

Keynes clearly thought workers would have a better standard of living if the currency was devalued or if workers consented to a reduction in money wage rates. These options would ensure that the resources of Britain were allocated to the best advantage among various industries, and between exports and production for the home market. But without devaluation and without adjustment of money wage rates there would be unemployment. Protection would reduce real wages and cause a less satisfactory distribution of productive resources than would occur after devaluation of the currency. However, if devaluation wasn't available, protection would ensure a higher level of employment than doing nothing—and, at the moment, increasing employment was the main objective.

Keynes understood the damage that would be done to other countries and to the global trading system if Britain were to act in a protectionist manner against the exports of those other countries. The risk of possible retaliation was also significant. But Keynes appears to have thought that this risk might be offset by a beneficial effect on the global financial system as a result of an increase in confidence in the City of London. Such a boost in confidence would be produced by an increase in macroeconomic activity and an increase in employment in Britain. He also thought that without an increase in employment Britain's ability to remain on the gold standard might come to be undermined because of a wish to devalue the currency, and that the resulting uncertainty would damage other countries and the global economic system.

Keynes was using protection as a substitute for devaluation. He knew and freely admitted that, for the reasons he had listed, protection was an imperfect substitute, but in theory it was the closest remedy to abandonment of the gold standard. Recall that Hume had stated that a decrease in British prices due to a decline in the quantity of money would make imports more expensive. A tariff would do the same. To approach the effect that Hume described, there would have to be both a uniform tariff on all imports and subsidies for exports. That was highly unlikely, and the introduction of selected tariffs would, Keynes noted, reduce economic efficiency. Still, though protectionism was heretical in one sense, it was consistent with what later happened.

Having made his protectionist point, Keynes moved on. In the last part of his five days of presenting evidence, Keynes returned to the quandary that Britain's position was condemning it to an unacceptably high level of unemployment. The remarkable remedy he proposed was a large increase in government expenditures on public works—what we now call a Keynesian expansion. This suggestion wasn't unprecedented; Keynes had published such a proposal in support of David Lloyd George in the run-up to the general election of 1929.

But Keynes failed to convince the committee that an increase in expenditures on public works wouldn't crowd out an equal amount of private expenditures. His fellow committee members were convinced that an increase in public expenditures would cause an equal reduction in private investment. Their argument was that public expenditures would have to be financed by the issuing of government bonds, which would compete with other financial assets. The competition for funds would ultimately displace the bonds that private firms wished to issue to fund their own private investments, *crowding out* the effects of government expenditures.

Keynes' failure to win this argument was clear to all who witnessed his interaction with Sir Richard Hopkins, a senior Treasury official who had been called by the committee to give evidence on crowding out. Hopkins' appearance led to a resumption of the debate between Keynes and the Treasury that had begun with the 1929 publication of *Can Lloyd George Do It?* (a pamphlet written by Keynes and Sir Hubert Douglas Henderson).

Hopkins repeatedly made it clear that he couldn't understand how crowding out could be avoided. Yet many years later it is hard to read Hopkins' testimony without becoming frustrated and feeling immense sympathy with Keynes. Hopkins' testimony steered warily between two alternatives. As a loyal civil servant, he couldn't let down Winston Churchill (the previous Chancellor of the Exchequer), who had commissioned a white paper criticizing *Can Lloyd George Do It?* And he also couldn't let down the new Chancellor of the Exchequer, who was undertaking a strictly limited scheme of public works.

When Keynes pressed him, Hopkins retreated in a carefully measured but entirely unsatisfactory way. A reference was made to the white paper that had criticized the increase in public works that Keynes was advocating. Hopkins assured the Macmillan Committee that the Treasury had never had a hard and fast position on the subject, although it clearly was opposed to the large expenditures that Keynes was advocating.

Keynes then asked if it was the Treasury position that "schemes of capital development are of no use for reducing unemployment." That, said Hopkins, was "going much too far." Keynes tried again, asking whether the Treasury really believed that any capital that could be found for such schemes would be diverted from other uses. That, said Hopkins, was a "much too rigid expression of any views that may have come from us." It was the "atmosphere in which schemes may be undertaken" that conditioned their consequences. Hopkins went on to say that the Treasury view wasn't a "rigid dogma." It was, he said, a "result of the view that we take as to the practical reactions of the scheme." Keynes, exasperated, said that it "bends so much that I find difficulty in getting hold of it." But Hopkins, not to be beaten, replied "Yes; I do not think these views are capable of being put in the rigid form of a theoretical doctrine."

Hopkins' replies in these exchanges were profoundly unsatisfactory, but Keynes was unable to convince the committee that Hopkins was wrong. The trouble was that Keynes' theory didn't help him to justify what he wanted to say. Keynes wanted to say that an increase in Bank rate would reduce investment, expenditures then would fall, and that would create unemployment. He also wanted to say that an increase in government spending wouldn't crowd out the investment of private-sector entrepreneurs. It would instead create more jobs and reduce the unemployment that had been created by the higher Bank rate. But his economic theory at this time didn't work that way, since the supply of output in the economy was assumed to be fixed. He wanted to say, and did say to the Macmillan Committee, that higher prices without wage increases would mean that production would become more profitable, and that this profit would induce capitalists to produce more and reduce unemployment. But his theory didn't allow him to say this. All it allowed him to say was that the increased government expenditures would increase the price of goods and depress the real income of workers, because wages would rise less than prices and crowd out the living standards of workers.

It is no wonder that Keynes and Hopkins disagreed on this issue. Their discussions were taking place in 1930 at a time of high and rising unemployment. A macroeconomic model that assumed that output was fixed at full-employment capacity wasn't particularly helpful. And the use of such a model to defeat Sir Richard Hopkins by arguing that public expenditures need not crowd out private investment expenditures because instead it would reduce workers' consumption was hardly helpful to Keynes.

Keynes' trouble was exactly parallel to his failure to show that an increase in Bank rate would cause a decrease in unemployment. If one assumes that output is always full employment, then an increase in government expenditures cannot cause an increase in employment—for exactly the same reasons that an increase in Bank rate cannot cause a decrease in employment.

At the end of these exchanges Lord Macmillan gave a judicial summary: "I think we may characterize it as a drawn battle." And Keynes wrote the following to his wife:

Sir R. Hopkins is very clever; but did not understand the technique of what we were discussing,—so the combination made a good hunt. But it proved that the Treasury don't know any more than the Bank of England what it is all about—enough to make tears roll down the eyes of a patriot."

Keynes may well have believed that the making of economic policy remained driven by the ideas of defunct economists at the Treasury and the Bank of England. But there was a fundamental incoherence in Keynes' advocacy of an increase in public works when his discussion of the gold standard had suggested that the country faced an external problem. Higher public expenditures would, he wanted to say, lead to an increase in employment and thus to an increase in domestic incomes and expenditures. But they also would cause an increase in imports, making the external problem worse. As a result, Keynes failed to persuade any other member of the Macmillan Committee to adopt his views.

4

Economics before Keynes, II: Marshall

It is hard to reconstruct Keynes' difficulties of 1930. We have sampled his writing and testimony since the First World War, and we continue by reviewing the state of economics at that time. Economists now divide their field into microeconomics (the study of individual markets) and macroeconomics (the study of economies as a whole), but this distinction did not exist before the Great Depression and Keynesian analysis. Instead, there was extensive microeconomics (brought to a kind of perfection under Alfred Marshall, Keynes' predecessor at Cambridge), and only the most cursory views of macroeconomics. We survey this older view briefly to indicate where Keynes started his innovative career and to show how his theories grew out of previous contributions.

One of the foundations of microeconomic analysis is the separation of supply and demand. We use supply and demand curves, and the graphs will carry over into Keynesian analyses. Both "supply" and "demand" refer to schedules or curves relating the quantity supplied or demanded as a function of the relevant price. We distinguish between supply and demand because it typically is the case that different people are behind them. Robinson Crusoe was both a supplier and a demander, of course, but it makes sense to distinguish him as a producer (providing a supply of a good) and a consumer (demanding the good). The distinction helps to clarify the role of different forces affecting the allocation of resources even in such a simple economy.

This separation began with Adam Smith. In one of his most famous passages (*The Wealth of Nations*, book I, chapter II), Smith asserted "It is not from the benevolence of the butcher, the brewer or the baker that we expect our dinner, but from their regard to their own interest." The sentence often is used as an expression of morality, but in this context it is a simple separation of supply from these tradesmen and demand from Smith or his readers. Smith had the concept of separating supply and demand, but he did not draw supply and demand curves. The graphical innovation was introduced by Antoine Cournot, a French mathematical economist, fifty years after *The Wealth of Nations*, and was popularized by Marshall in his *Principles of Economics* in 1890. A graph in which supply and demand curves are plotted together is often called a Marshallian Cross.

The interest in the determinants of crossing curves follows through into all the graphs presented in this book. The graphs provide a way to see how divergent interests coalesce into mutually beneficial arrangements—or sometimes fail to do so. We go from supply and demand to savings and investment, to product and financial markets, to internal and external balances. In each graph, the horizontal axes represent quantities that people, groups, or nations can change; the vertical axes usually represent a relevant price that helps the desired quantities of the varied participants to harmonize their desires.

These graphs are simple even though the world is complex. Economists typically invoke the Latin phrase *ceteris paribus*, meaning "other things being equal." In other words, they assume that everything else in the economy stays constant while only the variables in the graph change. This extension of Hume's thought experiment is a useful way to think, although we should remember when we come to apply the lessons of simple graphs to complex situations that other things may change.

In addition, the "curves" in these graphs are all straight lines. This is another simplification, used more in elementary macroeconomics than in Marshallian analysis. Any smooth curve can be approximated by a straight line, the approximation becoming less accurate as it extends further from the initial point. For clarity, most of the curves in this book appear to show large changes in economic conditions, but in fact we typically are describing small—what economists call marginal—adjustments. Using straight lines is a simplification, like drawing curves with only two variables. Even these simple models can provide great insights.

The quantity of a good or a service that is demanded generally increases when the price falls. At lower prices, people can consume more; their money (in whatever form it takes) goes farther. In addition, people often want more when the price is lower; they may shift between goods to use more of the cheapest goods and leave some money left over for other things. If prices get much lower, people may even think of new uses for a commodity. For example, the price of cotton fell dramatically during the Industrial Revolution, leading people to think of putting cotton sheets on the beds and cotton curtains on their windows.

These factors differ in intensity for different goods, and economists use the concept of *price elasticity* to describe the extent to which the quantity demanded rises when the price declines. Unitary elasticity is defined to be when the proportional increase in the quantity demanded just equals the proportional decline in the price. Total expenditure stays the same. When the quantity demanded changes less than this, the demand curve is inelastic; when it changes more, demand is elastic. Demand is infinitely elastic if it is so elastic that even a very small change in price will lead to dramatic—even infinite—changes in the quantity demanded. In that case, the very high elasticity of demand keeps the price from varying. That is true in competitive markets in which the actions of any single person have no effect on the price.

The quantity supplied generally increases when the price rises. As the price for a product increases, producers make and sell more. They can afford to use more inputs to produce their product, and they may enjoy greater return from the sale. The reasoning implicitly assumes that there are two inputs needed for production. Following a long tradition of classical economists, we call them labor and land. If land is fixed, then increasing the number of workers results in diminishing returns from each worker as more and more workers are added. It is diminishing returns that make the supply curve slope upward.

Supply and demand curves are illustrated in figure 4.1, where quantity is represented on the horizontal (x) axis and price on the vertical (y) axis. Since the demand curve slopes down and the supply curve slopes up, they generally cross. We identify the crossing point as the *equilibrium* in figure 4.1 because the demanders and the suppliers are agreed at this point to produce and consume this amount at the same price. There is no pressure to change, and the market can stay at this equilibrium indefinitely if the underlying curves do not shift.

What happens if the price is below that shown at the crossing point? The quantity of this good that producers want to sell is smaller than at the crossing point, while the quantity that people want to buy is larger than at the crossing point. The shortage of goods will enable producers to raise the price. As they do, this encourages them to supply more, and leads those who purchase the good to demand less. The price will rise as long as the price is below the price at the crossing point. Something similar happens if the price is above that shown at the crossing point: the price will fall as long as it is above that at the crossing point. Only when the price reaches this level will it neither rise nor fall, and only then will

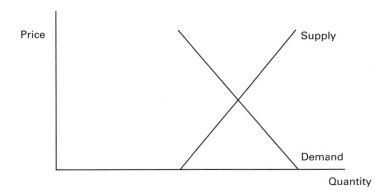

Figure 4.1
Supply and demand.

the quantity of the good which is sold remain unchanged. This is why we speak of the crossing point as the equilibrium position for this market.

How could the price have become low enough to set this process in motion? Figure 4.2 shows point B as a previous equilibrium with the same supply curve but a much lower demand curve. For example, we might be considering the market for people to shovel snow. When there is no snow, demand is low, and a big snowfall moves the demand curve sharply to the right. Alternatively, we might think of medical services. We generally do not go to a doctor when we are healthy; our demand curve is very low. But when we get sick, we want to see a doctor, and our demand for medical services rises. A rapid rise in the popularity of any item would have a similar effect, and this graph can be used for the analysis of many markets.

Figure 4.2 also illustrates a distinction critical to understanding these graphs. The shift of the demand curve causes movement along the supply curve. In other words, shifts of curves are distinct from movements along curves, and the direction of causation runs from shifts of curves to movements along curves. As was noted earlier, these curves show only part of a complex reality. We explain how changes outside our figures cause curves in the graphs to move, and we use the graphs to show how shifts in curves cause movements along curves. In figure 4.2, the shift in the demand curve leads to movement along the supply curve.

If there is a sudden expansion of demand, the dynamics may not be as simple as just described. Prices change more rapidly than quantities, and the shift in the demand curve may result initially in a rise in the price

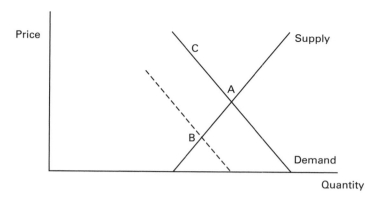

Figure 4.2
Shifting the demand curve.

before the quantity supplied can change. The price would have to absorb the initial shock of a higher demand, and it could rise further than the equilibrium price at A in figure 4.2. It could even rise to C where the new demand curve shows the amount demanded at the previous quantity. The new, high price then would stimulate suppliers to increase production, and the market would move from C to A. The initial spike in the price acts as a stimulus to speed movement from the old to the new equilibrium. We often speak of this kind of sudden price response as *overshooting*. (Economists also talk of "excess supply" when the price is above A, and of "excess demand" when the price is below A.)

What happens if the equilibrium is at A, as originally shown, but the price is restrained to stay at or below the level indicated by B? The price cannot move to C and then to A; it is stuck at B. The condition of excess demand described for B, that is, the condition where the demand for a product or service is higher than the supply, will continue. This is not an equilibrium, because neither suppliers nor demanders are happy. There will be pressure for change. Think about rent control—the classic case of price controls in cities where the demand for rent-controlled apartments is intense. People often then pay "key money" to induce current tenants to pass an apartment on to them. How much will they pay? The price indicated by point C in figure 4.2 shows the demand for the quantity of apartments at point B. That is the rental rate, masquerading as the price of keys, that clears this market. It is spoken of as the "shadow price" of a market that is present when the actual price is not free to move toward equilibrium.

Now think of a price that is above the equilibrium price, such as point C in figure 4.2. As before, if the price is "too high," then suppliers would see if they could sell off their unwanted inventories by reducing their prices, and prices would fall—ending, of course, at A. There is no overshooting in this scenario, since previously point C was an intermediate point in the progress from B to A. Now there is just a smooth transition down the demand curve to the equilibrium point.

Finally in our brief exploration of microeconomic analysis, consider what would happen if the demand curve, already low when it ran through point B in figure 4.2, fell so low that it did not cross the supply curve at a positive price. This condition is illustrated in figure 4.3. Any goods produced for this market would be worthless, and the supply curve would be purely notional. A negative price means that sellers pay consumers to take their goods from them. That surely is a losing proposition for any business; it can do better by not producing goods in the first place. The goods would vanish from the market. And since demand was so low, people would throw the worthless goods away; they had become rubbish. Instead of using a product for the purpose for which it was designed, people would consider only the cost of storage or disposal. At some later time, people might want old-fashioned goods as antiques or as keepsakes, and the demand curve would shift outward, crossing the supply curve again at a positive price. The price would rise above zero, and there would be new production. The revived market would be composed of both older and newer objects, perhaps even of genuine and fraudulent antiques.

This is not a book about rubbish, but figure 4.3 is very relevant to our exposition of Keynesian economics. It shows how curves can shift so far that the price cannot adjust to reach equilibrium. Prices are positive; they cannot go negative. If there were a pile of old magazines in your library, you would be very surprised to see a dollar bill tucked inside each of them. People buy things for positive prices, give away things that are not worth anything, and pay rubbish-disposal companies to take things away. No one advertises magazines for minus $5.

If we observe a condition like that illustrated in figure 4.3, we say that the market has failed. There is no market adjustment that will fix this market and create a new equilibrium. The goods and services represented in figures 4.1 and 4.2 have become waste material in figure 4.3. The point of rubbish theory was that some goods can go back and forth over time from furniture to rubbish and then antiques. Market failures such as that illustrated in figure 4.3 may be only temporary.

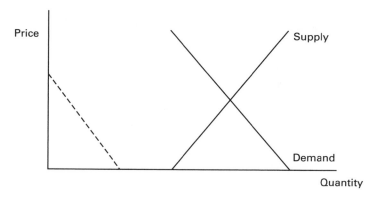

Figure 4.3
Rubbish theory.

In chapter 7 we describe a situation that looks like figure 4.3. Keynes argued that markets may cease to work properly in times of trouble. Workers in particular might find that there is not enough work to go around, and that many of them are unemployed. We will see that the interest rate might have to fall below zero to encourage people to spend more. But this cannot happen, just as the price in figure 4.3 cannot fall below zero. Unemployment can arise in this situation.

We can use supply and demand curves to see how Marshall and his followers analyzed the problem that Keynes grappled with during his presentations to the Macmillan Committee. To someone trained in the Marshallian tradition, the problem of unemployment was caused by trade unions and other institutions keeping the wage above the market clearing level, at a point like C in figure 4.2. At that level, the price for labor (that is, the wage) was above the equilibrium level. The amount of labor that workers would like to supply was larger than the amount of labor that business firms were willing to hire. More formally, the supply of labor exceeded the demand for labor at this high wage.

If wages were cut, this would increase the demand for labor because business firms would find it profitable to hire more workers. A wage cut also would reduce the supply of labor, since some workers would find it less desirable to find a job at the lower wage. This is how to understand Montagu Norman's position that the Bank of England had no effect on employment. He said that employment was determined by the wages set within each industry, which had nothing to go with Bank of England policy. If there was unemployment, the problem was that the wage was too high, that is, at point C in figure 4.2, above the wage that would provide full employment at point A.

The problem of an imbalance between savings and investment was analyzed similarly in the Marshallian tradition. Think again of figure 4.1. The price for savings and investment is taken to be the interest rate. (We explain why this is so in chapter 6.) At a high interest rate, people are eager to save, and the supply of savings slopes upward. The demand for investment by business firms would be low at a high interest rate because the firm would have to pay more to borrow funds to invest. The supply and the demand for savings and investment therefore look like those in figure 4.1, and the interest rate should move to equilibrate them.

Parallel to the analysis of the labor market, an interest rate above the equilibrium level would produce an excess supply of savings relative to the demand for investment. A decrease in the interest rate would lead to an equilibrium where the supply of savings equals the demand for investment. But in this Marshallian framework, there is no reason to think that an excess supply of savings would lead to a reduction in production, as Keynes had argued. In fact, in this framework, neither imbalances in the labor market nor imbalances in the market for savings and investment have any effect on aggregate production.

Observers using this framework would agree with Hopkins that the public works Keynes was advocating would be pointless. Public works would act like an increase in investment, shifting outward the demand for investments. That in turn would move the market up and to the right along the supply curve of savings. The rate of interest would rise. The increase in public works would crowd out private investment, leaving total production unmoved.

The possibility of low output of goods and of generalized unemployment that Keynes was trying to understand seemed impossible to someone trained in the Marshallian tradition. The Quantity Theory of Money told them that prices would adjust to make sure this did not happen. With a fixed quantity of money, prices were set by the demand curve for money. The higher price of goods, the more money would be demanded to finance all of the transactions in the economy. Prices therefore would settle at a level at which the quantity of money was just enough to enable all of the goods produced in the economy to be purchased, providing of course that these prices were flexible. As Keynes' discussion with Hopkins made very clear, Keynes had not yet seen how changes in prices did not ensure that everything produced in the economy would actually be purchased.

This Marshallian analysis all seems straightforward. The Marshallian tradition of microeconomics was very powerful. It is no surprise that Keynes had such difficulty while serving on the Macmillan Committee. He had not yet understood why cutting wages would not, by itself, reduce unemployment.

Later Keynes was able to show that cutting the wage would not increase employment because it would not lead to an increase in the demand for goods and an increase in the demand for labor to produce those goods. He was able to show that, instead, a cut in the wage on its own would lead to cuts in the prices of goods and would not make it any more profitable to employ labor. But Marshall's analysis could not help him to do this, since Marshall thought that the prices of goods were determined by the quantity of money.

Keynes had not yet understood why the interest rate did not ensure that all that is saved is automatically invested. He was later able to show that the interest rate did not fall in these circumstances. And he had not seen how changes in demand did not lead to changes in prices which went on ensuring everything produced in the economy was actually purchased.

To understand these things, Keynes had to understand that macroeconomics is more than just putting together microeconomic pieces. He had to understand that macroeconomics is about how markets interact with each other and prices and quantities are jointly determined. Keynes then had to see how this could be placed into a story about the open economy. Only then could he see a way to move beyond the view of an international economy that had been put forward by Hume in 1750 and championed by Norman in 1930.

5

The General Theory

We now turn to Keynes' approach to the two problems he faced at the end of 1930. He had failed to provide any alternative to the unsatisfactory workings of the gold standard. He consequently had failed to explain how a rise in Bank rate would increase unemployment and how expanding public works would reduce unemployment. He needed to rearrange his thinking to connect these apparently different questions.

Keynes opened his presentation to the Macmillan Committee with a description of how to maintain external balance under the gold standard. To make the argument—and to deal with the urgent demands on the committee—Keynes needed to confront the issue of domestic balance—that is, unemployment. Today we can distinguish these two interrelated issues because of contributions made by Keynes and many others after 1930. However, we cannot be sure that Keynes saw them as two separate questions. We can understand how working with one imbalance could exacerbate the other, but in 1930 Keynes lacked the tools to do this.

His innovations allowed him to answer both questions, but Keynes attacked the problems one at a time. Owing to the urgency of unemployment, Keynes chose to apply his insights to the domestic question first. That resulted in the publication of *The General Theory of Employment, Interest and Money* in 1936. Tackling the second question led to his important work on the creation of the International Monetary Fund at Bretton Woods in 1944—work that gave rise to the Swan diagram a decade later. By surveying these developments one at a time, we can follow the path of Keynes' intellectual progress.

Keynes approached his first daunting task by making some simplifying assumptions. He assumed a closed economy, meaning he would analyze each country as if it were the only country in the world. He also restricted himself to the short run, in which the capital stock is unchanging. He had made this assumption before, as our epigraph shows. Finally, he abandoned the assumption that prices are flexible which had been made by almost all previous economists—including by him in his *Treatise on Money*—for the more appropriate assumption for the 1930s: sticky prices. This assumption drew on his statement to the Macmillan Committee that wages could not be reduced, and it simplified Keynes' analysis in his first step. His assumption of sticky prices is appropriate when there is unemployment, but hardly when there is inflation. We do not assume that Keynes made all these assumptions explicit at once or even at the beginning of his intellectual journey, but rather that they emerged from the discussions of new ideas.

Keynes observed sticky wages, and many subsequent economists have tried to explain why wages do not fall in a recession. One appealing argument emerges from interviews of employers, who are very concerned about their employees' morale. Since it is prohibitively expensive to monitor every worker, employers try to inspire enthusiasm and trust in their employees to enhance their morale and induce them to work for the good of the company of their own volition:

Pay cuts damage morale, because of an insult effect and a standard of living effect. The latter occurs because a sudden decline in living standard distracts, depresses, and aggravates workers, and causes them to blame the company for their difficult adaptation to a lower income. ... The insult effect occurs because workers associate pay with self-worth and recognition of their value to the company. ... Hence a pay cut is interpreted as a signal of dissatisfaction with employees, even if everyone's pay is reduced.

Like many other economic arguments, this one amplifies thoughts found in Adam Smith. This argument sees *The Wealth of Nations* in the context of *The Theory of Moral Sentiments*, illustrating how Smith's two books support each other. Employers maximize their profits in society, and they rely on reciprocal social interactions to promote their economic activity.

Keynes' process of discovery started from his *Treatise on Money*. He was troubled by his inability to convince the Macmillan Committee using the analysis of the *Treatise*, which was published in October, 1930. In January of 1931, as the Macmillan Committee was drafting its report, a group of Keynes' young followers were meeting in Cambridge to discuss the *Treatise*'s strengths and weaknesses. That group, which included Austin and Joan Robinson, Piero Sraffa, James Meade, and Richard Kahn, became known as the Circus. Its first informal meetings were held in Kahn's rooms in Kings College. They were expanded into a more formal seminar held in the Old Combination Room at Trinity College, next door to Kings. Participation was strictly by invitation, and a few of the ablest undergraduates were invited after they had satisfied an interviewing board. Some research students and one or two other members of the teaching faculty sometimes attended. Keynes took no part in these activities, nor did Arthur Pigou, who had succeeded Marshall as Professor of Political Economy; he regarded such adolescent frivolities with Olympian detachment.

James Meade later enjoyed describing the meetings of the Circus. Although Keynes was not present, after each meeting Kahn saw Keynes and recounted to him the subject matter of the discussions and the lines of argument. "From the point of view of a humble mortal like myself," Meade noted, "Keynes seemed to play the role of God in a morality play; he dominated the play but rarely appeared on the stage. Kahn was the Messenger Angel who brought messages and problems from Keynes to the 'Circus' and went back to Heaven with the result of our deliberations." The casting of Keynes in this role was first suggested by Meade's wife in 1934 when they were staying with Austin and Joan Robinson in Cambridge. Messages from on high appeared at regular intervals during that weekend; God dominated the scene without making an appearance.

There is a lot of folklore about how the Quantity Theory of Money was abandoned. The most famous story involves a simple illuminating remark made by Austin Robinson, who contested the assumption in the *Treatise* that all adjustment is made by price changes: "If an entrepreneur, loaded with profits, decided on his way home to have a shoe-shine, was the effect solely to raise the price of shoe-shines? Was it impossible to increase the number of shoes shone?"

In the early 1930s, economists were used to dealing in prices, not quantities. They could deal with the quantity of any single good or service—Marshall had taught them how to do so. But when they came to think of the price level (that is, what we now call macroeconomics), they fixed the quantity of goods and services produced. That led to what we now call the Quantity Theory of Money. We saw this at the end of the last chapter. In order to free the analysis from the assumption of full employment, Keynes had to free himself from the Quantity Theory too.

Keynes made a start on the first of three needed innovations in his presentation to the Macmillan Committee by arguing that saving and investing were done by different people. The automatic equalization of saving and investment in the Quantity Theory disappeared. This freed Keynes to come up with a better framework, but at first it led to confusion. Keynes found a solution to his problem in the work of Richard Kahn, who had been studying how consumption is determined. And if the determinants of consumption are understood, then the behavior of savings is also understood, since savings simply equals income minus consumption.

Kahn had drafted his famous article on the *multiplier* by January of 1931. In that article he showed that if output is able to move in response to an increase in government expenditure, as in the discussions with Hopkins, an increase in investment or an increase in government expenditure can be brought back into line with savings by a rise in output, not by an increase in the interest rate. Such a rise in output will bring about an increase in profits because more people are brought into work, more goods are produced, and more goods are sold. There is some extra profit on each transaction. Output, said Kahn, will rise by just enough to make savings out of profits rise to match the increase in government expenditure. Output rises to bring savings back into line with investment again, rather than the interest rate rising enough to bring this about (as in Marshallian theory). This extra increase in output means that output will increase by more than the initial increase in government expenditure—hence the name by which it is still known: the multiplier.

Meade showed how Kahn's multiplier analysis could be connected with Keynes' previous argument in the *Treatise on Money*. Meade described his idea as follows:

I said the following to the other members of the Circus, "Haven't any of you read Marshall's *Principles of Economics*? In that book, in the short run, the economy lies on a short-run, upward-sloping, supply curve [as in figure 4.1]. But that curve adds an extra equation to the model. This means that—in comparison with the model in the *Treatise*—we can make *both* prices *and* output endogenous [able to move] at the same time."

Kahn acknowledged his debt to Meade in his article of 1931 and in his later account of the period. Once these ideas were understood, they led the Circus to the view that it is primarily variations in the level of *output* that bring savings into line with investment to re-establish the conditions of macroeconomic equilibrium.

Once quantities could change, Keynes needed to ask what caused them to change. His understanding of consumption followed from Kahn's ideas; he assumed that people's consumption varied primarily with their income. He formalized Adam Smith's observation that poor people consumed all their income just to keep alive. Rich people saved part of the income, and Keynes assumed that this part rose with income. The resulting *consumption function* showed consumption rising with income, but at a slower rate. Poor people consume all their income as they need to deal with their immediate concerns. In the language of economics, since personal savings are defined as the difference between income and consumption, the poor do not save. As income rises, people can save some of their income, and therefore saving rises with income. It was the consumption function that made Kahn's multiplier work. The resulting savings function is shown in figure 5.1.

The axes in figure 5.1 are different from those in our earlier graphs, but the similar shape helps to make this figure intelligible. The horizontal axis is a quantity, as in figures 4.1–4.3, but it is national production, not the production of a single commodity. The quantity of national production in the economy is equal to the income of all of those who work in the economy. Workers and capitalists are paid for the work they do, and they receive an income equal to the value of the national production they contribute to. We measure their incomes by the value of their production. We then measure national product by Gross Domestic Product (GDP), which is the quantity of goods and services produced in a country. Although GDP measures the quantity we want for the horizontal axis, we also refer to it as the national product, or even as national income (since that is equal to the value of what has been produced). These terms have slightly different meanings in other contexts, but here they are taken to be equal. The vertical axis represents the quantities of both savings and investments. At this stage of analysis, the quantity of investment is given by what Keynes later described as "animal spirits." Saving, however, depends on income. People save more as they become richer, and that is why the savings curve slopes upward.

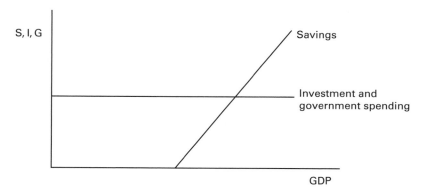

Figure 5.1
The Keynesian Cross.

A bit of simple bookkeeping may clarify figure 5.1. National income and national production are the same in this simple model, approaching the measurement of total output from two directions. The national income of citizens can be decomposed into consumption and savings. The production of firms and the government, measured by GDP, can be divided into consumption, investment, and government spending. As was noted above, the national income of citizens is equal to the production of firms and the government. Putting these two decompositions together implies that saving equals investment plus government spending. This is an identity, true at all times.

We can turn this identity into a simple economic model by specifying intended saving, intended investment, and government spending. Saving is determined by the consumption function. Recall that, according to the consumption function, consumption rises with income, albeit more slowly. This implies that the proportion of saving rises with income. Adding together the desired savings of everyone in the country, we get national savings as a function of national income. But since national income is the same as GDP—since national income is equal to the value of what has been produced—we get savings as a function of GDP. This procedure determines the slope of the line that represents savings in figure 5.1. For simplicity here, neither investment nor government spending is affected by the level of GDP.

The sum of intended investment and government spending, not dependent on GDP, appear as a horizontal line in figure 5.1—the same level for all levels of national product. Actual investment plus government spending, however, is equal to saving. From the identity just described, savings rise with national product. The difference between actual and intended investment is defined as *unintended investment*.

Because the Keynesian identity of savings and investments is true at all times, the dynamics of figure 5.1 can be expressed in terms of this continuing identity. The horizontal line shows intended investment rather than actual investment. When savings rise as shown in figure 5.2, production does not change immediately. Instead, investment rises to meet the new volume of savings at the existing level of income at point B. Since intended investment did not rise, it must have been unintended investment that rose.

Such unintended investment consists of the accumulation of unwanted inventories. Business firms produce goods for consumers to buy. When savings rise, consumption falls; people buy fewer goods. The unsold goods pile up as unwanted inventories. Companies see their inventories

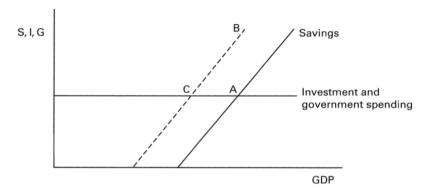

Figure 5.2
The Paradox of Thrift.

rise unexpectedly and reduce production to reduce their excessive inventories. The reduction of production decreases production and employment. The economy moves to the left in figure 5.2—toward the new intersection of savings and intended investment at point C.

Another type of unintended investment consists of empty buildings built at the end of a building boom. Investors may have been enthusiastically building homes and office buildings while demand was high. But with a decrease in demand, some of these buildings stand empty. Excessive inventories of buildings discourage further investment in new buildings.

Now Keynes could explain how the increase in savings could cause unemployment by using the multiplier. Consider a rise in savings as shown in figure 5.2. At the current level of GDP, savings exceed intended investment. Since spending is low, inventories build up. This is counted as investment, but businesses take an accumulation of unwanted inventory as a signal to reduce production. Output and income therefore fall. They fall until savings once again equal intended investment, since at that point inventories no longer are building up. This new equilibrium, shown by the intersection of the two lines at C in figure 5.2, is now at a lower level of income since the savings curve rose. The new equilibrium level of output does not require as much labor to produce it, so there is unemployment.

The dynamics of figure 5.1 are similar to those of figure 4.2. If the desire to save increases, the savings curve moves upward. The effect is to move the intersection where savings equals investment to the left in figure 5.2. Unlike Marshall's figures, figure 5.2 shows the equilibrium to be reached by the movement of GDP or national income and not by price changes. This graph is known as the *Keynesian Cross*, and the dynamics just described illustrate the *Paradox of Thrift*. The paradox is that the desire to save more does not increase savings; it decreases GDP. This figure is the essence of Keynesian economics in many people's minds. (We discuss the Paradox of Thrift further in chapter 7.)

The Keynesian Cross also can be drawn another way. The alternate presentation starts from consumption instead of savings. Since savings rise more rapidly than income, consumption must rise more slowly, as consumption and savings together equal income. As Adam Smith observed, poor people consume all their income and do not save; only when people have more income do they begin to save. If we graph consumption against income, it then starts positive and rises more slowly than income. Adding the other components of spending shown as a horizontal line in figure 5.1 yields total spending.

How do we know that this spending exhausts income, the same way that consumption and saving exhaust income? We plot production against production by drawing a 45-degree diagonal line that is the same distance from the horizontal axis as it is from the vertical axis. Where the line for total desired spending crosses the 45-degree line, desired spending equals actual spending. At any other level of income, desired spending is more or less than actual spending, and there will be undesired investment or undesired disinvestment. More concretely, inventories will rise or fall. This will lead producers to change production to bring inventories back to their desired level, changing the level of production until the level at which the two curves cross is reached. This presentation of the Keynesian Cross, therefore, is equivalent to the one in figure 5.1. It shows the same equilibrium, and it has the same dynamics that make this equilibrium stable. The difference is that this version starts from consumption, whereas figure 5.1 starts from saving. We chose to use figure 5.1 to express the Paradox of Thrift as a simple increase in desired saving. This means, of course, that people reduced their consumption, which is how the Paradox of Thrift is shown in the alternate version.

The Paradox of Thrift is important because it shows why governments are different from families. Governments can borrow as long as investors will buy their bonds. Only when governments cannot borrow are they like poor families, who have to balance their budgets every year. In the US, the individual states are like poor families because they have constitutional provisions against borrowing. The federal government, however, has borrowed successfully for more than 200 years.

How can we get back to full employment? Consumers and business firms are not spending enough. The only entity that can spend more is the government. Keynesian policy calls for the government to take up the slack and reduce unemployment by spending more, as illustrated in figure 5.3. Unhappily for the world in 2014, policy makers in Europe and America have forgotten this simple Keynesian lesson. If government spending rises, the horizontal line (representing investment plus government spending) no longer crosses the savings function where it did before. Savings have to rise to get to a new equilibrium, and production has to rise to make savings rise. (This is not the end of the story. In a fuller model, taxes have to be added to government spending. In the case just described, the government does not change taxes or borrowing. We do not have bonds in this model, so we cannot see the effect of bonds here. We will present a fuller model in chapters 6 and 7; this model, however, is appropriate for conditions in 2014.)

In figure 5.3, the new equilibrium level of GDP at the intersection of the new curves is higher than the old equilibrium, showing the effect of fiscal policy through increased government spending. The increase in spending is shown by the vertical distance between points A and B. The increase in the GDP is represented by the horizontal distance between points B and C. The multiplier is the ratio of these two distances. A flatter savings function yields a higher multiplier. Keynes expressed this conclusion in characteristically colorful prose:

For a man who has been long unemployed some measure of labour, instead of involving disutility, may have a positive utility. If this is accepted, the above reasoning shows how 'wasteful' loan expenditure may nevertheless enrich the community on balance. Pyramid-building, earthquakes, even wars may serve to increase wealth, if the education of our statesmen on the principles of the classical

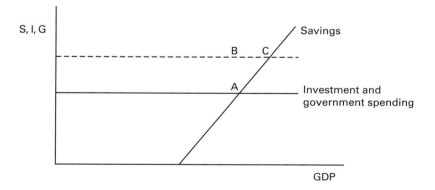

Figure 5.3
Fiscal expansion.

economics stands in the way of anything better. ... If the Treasury were to fill old bottles with banknotes, bury them ... and leave it to private enterprise ... to dig the notes up again ... there need be no more unemployment. ... It would, indeed be more sensible to build houses and the like; but if there are political and practical difficulties in the way of this, the above would be better than nothing.

Neither money nor the interest rate appears in these stories of the Keynesian Cross and the multiplier. We implicitly assume at this point that the interest rate is unchanged. Keynes acknowledged that the interest rate was important both in his introduction to the Macmillan Committee and in his argument with Hopkins, but he approached his new theory slowly. These primitive tools, therefore, are useful only when it is safe to assume that the interest rate is unchanged.

Consider conditions in 2014. As a result of the Global Financial Crisis of 2008, the prices of houses and of mortgage-backed securities have gone way down. Consumers lost a lot of wealth and are consuming less than they once had. In other words, they are saving more. Business firms lost a lot of their capital—since they are holding depreciated financial assets based on depreciated housing assets—and they too are spending less. Since they are spending less, they are saving more. The savings line in figure 5.2 moved far upward. In fact, the decline in spending has been so large that the interest rate has fallen to zero.

Another form of fiscal policy should be acknowledged here. Keynes emphasized expanding government spending, but reducing taxes also can increase national production. Cutting taxes is a less effective macroeconomic tool than adding to government spending because it acts indirectly; people need to react to tax cuts to change national income. Cutting taxes for low-wage workers leads them to spend more to increase their consumption. Cutting taxes for high-wage workers has a smaller effect on the economy because high-wage people save added income instead of spending it. In America today, only reducing taxes for low-wage workers comes close to expanding government spending as effective fiscal policy.

Keynes had abandoned Marshall's analysis and adopted a new one. Figure 4.2 illustrates Marshall's assumption that prices move to equilibrate the market for goods and services to get to the equality of supply and demand. Figure 5.1 illustrates Keynes' assumption that national income, and thus GDP, moves to equilibrate the market for goods and services to get to the equality of savings and desired investment. Marshall assumed that prices were flexible; Keynes assumed that they were fixed. Marshall assumed that anyone who wanted to work could find a job; Keynes assumed that there could be involuntary unemployment.

In order to deal with the increasing unemployment that was evident in 1930, Keynes had to introduce unemployment into his thinking. He could not deal with both a changing demand for labor and flexible prices, despite Meade's urging, and he concentrated only on the former. This enabled him to originate the field we now call macroeconomics. The Paradox of Thrift comes about because there is a difference between everyone wanting to save more and the inability of the economy as a whole to absorb more savings. This adding-up problem did not occur in Marshall's analysis.

Keynes' new approach—macroeconomics—also led to a new meaning for the word "unemployment." In the largely agricultural economies of the nineteenth century, people were employed in a yearly cycle that did not vary with economic conditions. Unemployed workers either could not or would not work; we call them, in retrospect, voluntarily unemployed. Keynes, by contrast, was describing conditions in which workers wanted to work but could not find jobs. They were involuntarily unemployed. This kind of unemployment emerged at the end of the nineteenth century, when workers migrated to cities to work in large factories. And Keynes showed how the Paradox of Thrift could lead to a shortage of jobs for workers looking for jobs. The meaning of unemployment changed to describe a new condition that came to be called involuntary, or Keynesian, unemployment.

Keynes was the first to argue that involuntary unemployment represented a failure in the product market, not a failure in the labor market. The problem did not lie in negotiations about wages or hours; it lay in the inability of hiring firms to sell their products. That, in turn, was the result of an excess of savings that reduced GDP. This lesson should be remembered today in the depressed conditions that have followed the world financial crisis of 2008. People are unemployed because there are not enough jobs—not because they belong to unions or because they have demanded higher wages. The way to get to full employment is to fix the product market as described in this chapter, not to blame workers for their unhappy condition.

This new way of thinking emerged from the simplest of models. Keynes deviated from his description of the gold standard to the Macmillan Committee to break decisively with tradition. The Keynesian Cross built on the consumption function to create a new way to analyze a whole economy. There are no prices in the Keynesian Cross—neither the price of goods in money nor the price of money itself.

Keynes' new model enabled him to turn economics on its head, but it is applicable to economic policy only in special circumstances. Money and bonds do not appear in the Keynesian Cross, and the model does not explain the determinants of investment and government deficits. Foreign transactions also are absent, and the model does not integrate its insights with Keynes' concern about the gold standard. However, the Keynesian Cross is sufficient to provide guidance when the interest rate has fallen to its lower bound of zero and when a government controls prices directly in wartime. (We expand the Keynesian model in the next chapter to include domestic money and bonds; we expand it further in chapter 8 to include foreign money and bonds.)

A decade after Keynes died, in the midst of the economic boom that followed the Second World War, Robert Solow and Trevor Swan each adopted the framework of figure 5.1 (that is, a Keynesian saving function), but returned to Marshall's assumption of full employment to consider long-run economic growth. Solow and Swan assumed that investment would change in response to a shift in the savings function. Instead of producing unemployment, a rise in the savings function produces more investment and so more capital accumulation. It therefore leads to more output and to the possibility of more consumption in the future. The combination of a Keynesian savings function and Marshallian equilibrium led to what is now called the Solow-Swan model of economic growth and to the founding of a new subfield of economics about economic growth. Note that Keynesian unemployment does not appear in the Solow-Swan model. In that respect, the Solow-Swan model is closer to Marshall than to Keynes. The aim of Solow and Swan was to focus on the long run. In the long run, the fluctuations of employment that motivated Keynes appear as deviations around demographically determined labor inputs.

We can illustrate this difference by recalling figure 4.1. The Solow-Swan model argues that the level of GDP is determined in the long run by shifts of a curve representing *aggregate supply*. For example, the difference in the levels of GDP in the United States and Britain between the times of Hume and even Marshall and today are the results of expanding aggregate supply curves. By contrast, the Keynesian Cross argues that the level of GDP is determined in the short run of a few years by shifts in the level of *aggregate demand*.

6

IS-LM Curves

How can a government be sure that its increased spending would not be offset by a decrease in private spending? This was one of the questions Keynes could not answer during his presentation to the Macmillan Committee. Keynes had made important steps, but he still lacked a good answer to Hopkins.

Keynes needed to expand his model of the Keynesian Cross to include the interest rate. The graphs in chapter 5 did not have any prices in them; they were based on the consumption function that related national consumption and production. This simple model produced insights like the Paradox of Thrift, but it could not answer all the questions that Norman and Hopkins raised in the Macmillan Committee. To find answers, Keynes expanded his model to include the rate of interest. Norman had acknowledged that central banks affected interest rates. Keynes took that seriously, but he parted with Norman by arguing that interest rates affected the quantity of production—an extension Norman had denied.

In order to make this argument, Keynes simplified his treatment of financial markets to focus on the effects of finance on expenditures. He assumed there was only one interest rate in his model economy. Keynes had followed Marshall's lead in generalizing from an analysis of an individual's consumption functions to a national consumption function. Keynes was a successful investor; he knew the complications of buying and selling stocks and bonds, with their many different rates of return. But as an economist he was not describing the financial sector in detail; he was trying to explain how the financial sector affects real expenditures.

The restriction to a single interest rate implies that there is a single interest-bearing asset—a single bond. The interest rate in the expanded Keynesian model then was the rate of return of this bond. This too was a simplification. The unitary bond represented the whole range of bonds— from short-term government obligations affected by central banks to long-term industrial bonds issued as business firms financed their investments. As with the interest rate, it is important to remember that the Keynesian model is a model of the economy, not a description. The simplifications in the model come at the cost of detailed reality; the gain is an understanding of how the economy works.

The interest rate on this single bond provides the link to connect financial actions to decisions about the production and consumption of goods. Keynes understood the importance of this link, and he made a strategic decision. He modeled the supply of and the demand for money with which people bought bonds, but he did not model the supply of and the demand for bonds. Money is far more homogeneous than bonds, and this decision to focus on the demand and supply of money enabled Keynes to focus on the connection between finance and production.

Letting the quantity of production and employment vary instead of prices had made possible the first breakthrough Keynes needed to make to escape from Marshall's Quantity Theory of Money. This was the observation that savings are decided by households' deciding how much of their income to consume and how much to put aside for the future, summarized in a consumption function. As we saw in chapter 5, this insight enabled Keynes to describe how the consumption function determined the level of production and how an excess of savings could lead to the Paradox of Thrift.

Investment is determined by firms when they decide how much capital equipment they need for production and how much they must invest in order to get this capital equipment. This investment need is dependent on animal spirits, which results in the horizontal line of figure 5.1 representing the sum of unexplained government expenditures and unexplained investment. Neither of these magnitudes is affected by the level of production in the simple model of chapter 5, which is why the line is horizontal—the same for any level of income.

In his expanded model, Keynes argued that investment was dependent on the rate of interest in addition to animal spirits. Just as individuals save more when incomes are high, businesses invest more when the rate of interest is low. Keynes called the demand curve for investment as a function of the interest rate, the second of his three innovations, the *marginal efficiency of capital*.

To see what this means, suppose that you own a factory that earns a steady income of 5 percent on your investment. Assume first that the interest rate falls to 2 percent. You can borrow money at 2 percent and add to your factory earning 5 percent. Instant money! At that low interest rate, you are happy to invest more. Now assume that the interest rate rises to 8 percent. You are now unhappy. You can buy a bond earning 8 percent instead of investing in your factory that earns only 5 percent. You will neglect your factory or even try to sell it, since you can earn more money with the money you save. In short, lower interest rates encourage you to invest in your factory, and higher interest rates discourage you from doing so.

In the discussion of figure 5.3 in chapter 5, we regarded the upward shift of the investment and government spending line as coming from an increase in government spending. Now let us think of it as a rise in investment due to a lower interest rate. In other words, the solid line that led to the equilibrium at A was for a certain interest rate. The dashed line shows the increased level of investment at a lower interest rate. Looking to see where the higher investment and government spending line crosses the savings line, we see that the economy has moved to point C at a higher level of national income. A lower interest rate has led to an increase in national income.

Keynes had enlarged his model by introducing the marginal efficiency of capital. As was discussed in chapter 5, only national production and savings changed in the Keynesian Cross. Now Keynes was able to consider how movements in the rate of interest can cause movements in national production. We can draw a graph to display this idea, putting the interest rate on the vertical axis while retaining GDP on the horizontal axis. This new line shows different positions where savings equals intended investment plus government expenditures for different interest rates. It slopes downward in this graph. This new idea was the second of the breakthroughs which Keynes needed to escape from Marshall's Quantity Theory of Money. (The first breakthrough was the consumption function.)

These two breakthroughs meant that if one could understand the determinants of savings and investment decisions at any interest rate, one could understand how expenditures, output, and employment were likely to change. This involved a major revision in the way anyone thought about how the economy works. But Keynes needed to make a third and equally fundamental move before he could dispense with the objections Hopkins had raised. If the amount of total spending in the economy was determined by the balance between savings and investment at any interest rate, what determined the rate of interest? Why doesn't the rate of interest just move to ensure that savings equals investment when all resources are fully employed, as Marshall had assumed? For Keynes, money and finance in the economy can play a part in preventing this from happening.

To show this, Keynes had to clarify the role of the quantity of money in the economy. This was his third breakthrough.

Keynes made this move by considering the supply of and the demand for money, using figure 4.1 to analyze the market for money in the same way it could represent the supply of other goods. The price of money in this background graph is of course the rate of interest. The supply of money is determined by central banks, as Norman had argued. Central banks change the supply of money by buying and selling bonds. When a central bank buys bonds, it increases the supply of money in the private economy. When it sells bonds, it reduces the supply of money in private hands.

These purchases and sales are known as *open market* purchases and sales (or open-market operations) because they are made on the open market. Although there is only one kind of bond in this model, Keynes assumed that there were enough potential buyers to make a competitive market. Looking at the graphs in this book, it is easy to forget that they represent a simplified model of a large economy. We invoke this large-economy idea to support the assumption of a competitive bond market even though this market and the many potential purchasers and sellers do not appear explicitly in the model.

Turning to the demand side, Keynes described two uses of money. The first use of money is as a means of payment. If there are more goods and services in an economy or if prices are higher, then more money is needed to grease the wheels of commerce. Keynes called this demand for money a *transaction demand*. Left alone, the demand for money as a means of payment—the transaction demand—leads to the Quantity Theory of Money. In the Keynesian model, however, this is only one of the reasons that people hold money.

A second reason to hold money, Keynes argued, was for speculation. If interest rates are low, then the price of bonds is high; the price and the yield of bonds move in opposite directions. Think of a $100 bond paying a dividend of $10 a year. If the price of the bond falls by half, whoever buys it for $50 gets the same yield which is now one-fifth of the price, no longer one-tenth. The interest rate has increased from 10 percent to 20 percent. People are reluctant to buy bonds at high prices; they prefer to hold their resources in cash—in money—to speculate that bond prices will fall and become more attractive to buy. If interest rates are high, then the price of bonds is low. If interest rates are high, the cost of holding money relative to the return which would be earned by instead holding bonds, that is, the interest rate, is high as well. People buy bonds—buying low in the hope of selling high—to speculate that the price of bonds will rise, that the interest rate will fall. Keynes called this demand for money *liquidity preference*: a wish to hold assets in "liquid" form—that is, in money—in order to use this money to speculate by buying bonds when the time seems right to do so.

Liquidity preference is the demand for money for speculative purposes. The demand for money depends both on GDP (transaction demand) and the rate of interest (liquidity preference). The rate of interest is the common rate for all bonds in this model, from short-term government bills to long-term industrial bonds. And the supply of bonds in the background is implicitly assumed to be what is necessary to fund private investment and any government deficit. This is parallel to the Keynesian assumption of fixed supply of money.

An increase in the quantity of money in this model causes the interest rate to fall. This is because wealth holders now have too much money in their portfolios of bonds and money. They buy bonds to rebalance their portfolios, increasing the price of bonds and decreasing the interest rate. The interest rate is determined in this story by the need to make the demand for money equal to the supply of money, not by the need to make savings equal to investment. The story is simple. The demand for money depends on the rate of interest as well as on the number and size of transactions for which people need money.

Some people wish to hold their wealth in the form of liquid money if they are unsure whether the price of bonds or shares is going to go up or down. We know this from our experience at the end of 2008, when traders wanted cash for their bonds after the bankruptcy of Lehman Brothers. Followers of Alfred Marshall knew this too. In times of crisis, the risk of failure makes the value of bonds decline and leads bondholders to sell bonds to get cash. That will cause the interest rate to rise, since those holding a bonds get the same interest payments even although they obtain the bonds for less money, so that that return on the bond rises. It is the rush to sell bonds that causes a panic, revealed by the sudden rise in interest rates.

This story shows why conditions in the money market can cause the rate of interest to rise. This in turn can prevent the interest rate from ensuring that savings equals investment at a level of output at which there is full employment of resources. When wealth holders change their minds and sell bonds, this raises the interest rate. Those who borrow to invest have no alternative but to borrow at a higher rate of interest; they will invest less. Output and employment will fall. This is why Marshall was mistaken.

This idea had not been brought into the analysis of how an economy works as a whole. Keynes brought this idea into the determination of output and employment. It became known as his theory of liquidity preference, a theory that resulted from the idea that some of the reasons that people want to hold money are related to their wish to have a liquid asset, rather than having all of their money tied up in long-dated bonds or in shares, since these assets might happen to have a low price at just the time they have to be sold to finance an expenditure. If that is how some of the demand for money is determined, then the interest rate will make the supply of money (controlled by the central bank) equal to the overall demand for money, including both the demand that people have for money for transactions purposes and this additional liquidity demand.

We separated these two motives for holding money in order to understand how liquidity preference can be combined with the expanded relation of savings and investment in a model that includes both the national product and the interest rate. Liquidity preference argues that people hold money in case there is some reason they want to spend it. In other words, they want liquidity. How much money will people hold for this purpose? If money were free, everyone would hold unlimited amounts to be ready for any good or bad break. But money is not free. Money held for liquidity is not invested in an interest-earning bond. The cost of holding money is the forgone interest from owning a bond. At a higher interest rate, the cost is higher. People decide how much money to hold for liquidity at each interest rate. This leads them to hold less money for liquidity. It is a simple move up a demand curve like that shown in figure 4.1.

The demand for money for transactions is in addition to the liquidity demand for money. The two kinds of money demand may not be completely independent of each other, but it is helpful to consider them separately. A large economy—one with a higher level of GDP—will need more money at any given price level for transactions. As the economy moves from A to C in figure 5.3, the transaction demand for money will rise. In other words, the demand for money is a function of both the interest rate and GDP.

How will these demands for money interact with both the interest rate and the level of GDP? The supply of money is fixed by the central bank in this model. Start with an assumed agreement between the supply of and the demand for money at a particular interest rate. Then assume that the level of GDP rises for some reason. If nothing else happens, the demand for money exceeds the supply. This will cause people to sell bonds to obtain money to finance their transactions. As a result, the interest rate will rise, reducing the speculative demand for money, and restoring the previous equality of supply and demand for money. In order to maintain equilibrium in the money market—where supply and demand for money are equal—GDP and the interest rate must rise and fall together. We can draw a graph to display this idea, putting the interest rate on the vertical axis and GDP on the horizontal axis. The curve of equilibria for different levels of GDP slopes upward.

We now have two curves in a graph of with the interest rate on the vertical axis and GDP on the horizontal axis. The first curve shows points where savings equal investment. It slopes downward as explained a few paragraphs ago; a lower level of the interest rate leads to a higher level of GDP. Since the curve refers to investment and savings, we call it the IS curve. The second curve shows points where the demand and supply of money are equal. It slopes upward; a higher level of national income leads to a higher interest rate. Since it shows the interaction between liquidity preference and the money stock, we call it the LM curve. They are both shown in Figure 6.1.

John Hicks published the IS-LM diagram shown here as figure 6.1 a year after *The General Theory of Employment, Interest and Money* appeared. It was used widely after the Second World War to explain Keynesian analysis, although a simple graph cannot hope to capture the subtleties of Keynes' book. It made the often tortuous arguments of Keynes' book accessible to many students, and we use it here to summarize Keynesian thought for a single economy. (Hicks argued late in life that the IS-LM model was his own theory, not Keynes'. But even though Hicks carefully articulated how his theory differed, the IS-LM diagram lives on as a representation of Keynesian thought.)

Figure 6.1 looks like figure 4.1, but the labels are different. As in figure 5.1, the horizontal axis represents national production or GDP, often represented by economists as Y. The vertical axis represents the interest rate. There is no distinction between the real interest rate and the nominal interest rate as prices are assumed constant.

The IS curve represents equilibrium points in the markets for goods and services. It is an extension of figure 5.1, making investment a function of the interest rate. As the interest rate falls, investment rises. Investment will now be higher than saving. Production and income will rise until savings are again equal to investment.

The LM curve represents equilibrium in the money market. The LM curve shows different combinations of the interest rate and GDP where wealth holders are content to hold a given quantity of money and there are no pressures for the interest rate to change. As GDP rises, the demand

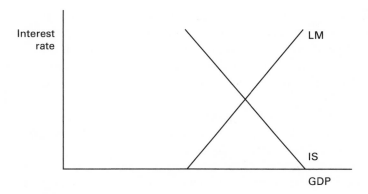

Figure 6.1
The IS-LM diagram.

for money rises. The interest rate must rise to ensure equilibrium in the money market.

The IS curve shows different combinations of the interest rate and national product where savers and investors are content, and at which firms do not wish to change their level of production. The LM curve shows different combinations of the interest rate and national income where wealth holders are content to hold a given quantity of money. Where the curves cross, both groups are content, and there is no pressure to change either the interest rate or GDP.

The equilibrium in figure 6.1 is based on the preferences of separate groups of people, as in figure 4.1. In this case, the same people or business firms may be making investments and holding money, but we think of these two activities as separate. As we explained in chapter 1, we can think of Robinson Crusoe as both a producer and a consumer; here, however, we think of these businessmen and women separately as they make separate decisions. Turning to consumers in figure 6.1, we can think of consumers as making two decisions as well. They decide how much of their income to save—that is, how much of their income not to consume—and whether they want to hold their savings in money or bonds.

How does this IS-LM analysis change the argument for fiscal expansion in the last chapter? Figure 5.3 described the multiplier effect of a fiscal expansion when the interest rate remained unchanged. This conclusion needs to be modified when the interest rate is free to change.

An increase in government spending appears as a shift to the right of the IS curve in figure 6.1. As GDP rises, the demand for money rises too (for added transactions) and people will sell bonds. This will drive down the price of bonds, increasing the rate of interest. That has two effects. The rise in the interest rate reduces the liquidity demand for money and keeps the economy on the LM curve. The rise in the interest also reduces the demand for investment and lowers the impact of the fiscal expansion. This lower impact is what Hopkins meant by "crowding out."

It is clear that the extent of crowding out is determined by the slope of the LM curve, by the elasticity of the demand for money. The multiplier in figure 5.3 will not be observed if the demand for money is inelastic (that is, steep in figure 6.1). This has made it hard for economists to agree on the size of the multiplier because the LM curve varies in its steepness over the course of the business cycle. It is very flat when the economy is depressed and steep when the economy is running at full capacity.

After his three breakthroughs, Keynes' new theory added up to the following set of beliefs. Keynes believed that the amount of investment in the economy depended on the opportunities for investment and on the rate of interest. As in his discussion of the short-run part of the gold-standard mechanism, a rise in the interest rate causes the level of investment to fall. But how is the rate of interest determined? Keynes' answer was: primarily by the quantity of money. Reducing the supply of money will cause the interest rate to rise. The Bank of England is able to make Bank rate rise by reducing the quantity of money available. What determines the overall level of expenditure and output in the economy? That depends on finding the level of output that will make savings out of incomes big enough to be equal to investment. If, say, investment falls, then this will cause a reduction in the incomes of those working to make goods that are sold for investment purposes, and so the amount that people can spend will fall. As a result, income and output will fall. Savings will fall until the point is reached at which savings are again equal to investment. Finally, what determines the level of employment in the economy? It is not determined by the wage at all! It is determined by the level of output because that determines how many people entrepreneurs will want to employ to make the output that they are able to sell. This, in a nutshell, is the view put forward by Keynes in his *General Theory*.

The IS-LM diagram we have presented in figure 6.1, which was published by John Hicks in 1937, adds a further important dimension to the above story. If the Bank of England holds the quantity of money fixed, then the level of output in the economy will influence the demand for this money. That will exert an influence on the rate of interest. As a result, the argument put forward in the last paragraph becomes just one part of a more general, simultaneous argument. The rate of interest influences the level of output, and the level of output influences the rate of interest.

The preceding sentence summarizes what generations of undergraduates have been taught about Keynes' *General Theory*. It comes from a discussion between Keynes and Roy Harrod in August of 1935, when *The General Theory* was in proofs. Harrod put Keynes' theory as clearly as anybody had done up until that point in time, and exactly as we put it above. Keynes categorically agreed with Harrod's interpretation. The view described in the previous two paragraphs is the one that came to prevail, and we think it is the correct one. This is not to deny that Keynes was aware that his theory had many limitations, and not to deny that he was not aware of many ways in which it could be extended. (In chapter 8 we discuss the generalization of the analysis to an economy that has international trade.)

The IS-LM diagram enabled Keynes to answer Norman and Hopkins. Norman had insisted that changing the interest rate did not affect production and employment. It is clear from figure 6.1 that if the Bank of England decreased the supply of money so that the interest rate would rise for any level of output. This means that the LM curve moves upward. As a result, the economy would move up and to the left along the IS curve. National income and employment would fall. This is the second stage of the adjustment to a loss of gold that Keynes had presented to the Macmillan Committee, which he could now explain to Norman.

Hopkins had asserted that increasing government spending would completely crowd out private investment and would not affect GDP or employment. We see from figure 6.1 that if government spending increases, the IS curve moves to the right. This moves the economy up and to the right along the LM curve. The higher level of the interest rate means that the economy will move up and to the left along the new IS curve; there will be less investment and so output will be lower than it otherwise would have been. Hopkins had a point, but he did not understand how or when it was relevant. He asserted that added government spending would not have any effect, but although the increase in national product is not as large as if the interest rate had not risen, it is clearly positive. As shown in figure 6.1, the severity of crowding out depends on the slope of the LM curve. The interest rate has to rise to crowd out private investment, and the amount of crowding out is determined by the extent to which the interest rate rises. Only if the LM curve is vertical is crowding out complete.

James Meade was nervous about the LM curve on the grounds that central banks do not actually determine the stock of money, and many others have been nervous about that too. Central banks play a prominent role in determining the stock of money, but other factors should be considered. A recent innovation has been to replace the LM curve with a curve representing central-bank policy and labeled MP (standing for "monetary policy"). If the central bank raises the interest rate when employment is high and lowers it when unemployment is high, the resulting MP curve slopes upward like the LM curve. Since the analysis is not affected by this modern restatement, we stay with the familiar representation of the money market.

Whether we use the LM curve or the MP curve, open-market purchases by the central bank shift the curve to the right. Both curves enable us to move away from Hume's purely metallic money supply to a fiduciary standard. The LM curve relies on the nature of the demand for money to get its positive slope; the MP curve gets its positive slope because of the policy which the central bank uses to set the interest rate. This difference may be important in more complex macroeconomic models, but it need not concern us here.

7

The Liquidity Trap

The Keynesian revolution changed our understanding of how the economy works. One way to understand the Keynesian revolution is to ask what happens if there is unemployment and wages are cut. According to Alfred Marshall, this makes firms demand more labor and reduce unemployment, an effect on unemployment that is magnified if some people decide to work less when the wage falls. According to Keynes, the reduction in wages reduces unemployment only if it leads to a reduction in the interest rate that stimulates more investment, or to a reduction in the amount of their income that people want to save. Only then will investment rise above savings, the level of expenditure and output rise, and unemployment fall. If this does not happen, then the fall in wages would just cause firms to lower their prices, rather than encouraging them to take on any new labor. Firms will take on new labor only if they can see an increased demand for their products.

The new macroeconomic method of analysis gives a sense of how macroeconomic outcomes are determined in more than one market at a time as part of a *general equilibrium* for the economy as a whole. Alfred Marshall did not understand this method. For Marshall, prices were determined by money, and the interest rate was determined by what was needed to make people invest what they saved. The wage was determined to make the demand for labor equal to the supply of labor. The microeconomic method Marshall used says the following: First figure out which market you talking about, then figure out how the price is determined in that market to make demand equal to supply. If you are thinking about the labor market, then the wage is determined to make the demand for labor equal to the supply of labor. Unemployment comes about only because wages are too high, and unemployment can be removed by cutting wages. If you are thinking about the goods market, the interest rate is determined to make savings equal to investment.

If there is a reduction in investment, then the interest rate will simply fall enough to make investment rise again, and/or make savings fall so that savings and investment come to be equal to each other again, and there will never be a shortage of the demand for goods. And if you are thinking about the money market, the price level is determined to make the demand for money equal to the supply of money. If the quantity of money is increased then that will cause the level of prices to rise—because people will spend more for goods and bid up prices. Similarly, if the quantity of money is reduced, then prices will fall. A decrease in the quantity of money does not cause an increase in unemployment.

Keynes escaped from such a confined way of thinking in *The General Theory of Employment, Interest and Money*. For Keynes, the amount of employment is determined by the level of GDP in the economy. The level of GDP is the one at which the level of savings equals the level of investment. It is not the case that the wage is determined to make the demand for labor equal to the supply of labor. Similarly, the interest rate doesn't simply make savings equal to investment. And the price level is determined by the level of wages, not by the quantity of money. As we say to our students: macroeconomics is the study of a subject in which everything depends on everything else. But good macroeconomics requires understanding which bit of everything influences which other bit of everything else in the most important way. That is why macroeconomics is such a challenging subject. Keynes led the way in showing economists, and the wider public, how to think in a macroeconomic manner.

Paul Samuelson understood that Keynes' *General Theory* was what economists call general-equilibrium theory in which there is a connection between markets in the way that we have just described. The postwar generation learned the Keynesian model from Samuelson's famous textbook *Economics*. Samuelson used the Keynesian Cross, but he did not use IS-LM curves—perhaps because interest rates were fixed in the late 1940s.

Think now about the conditions that have prevailed since the Global Financial Crisis of 2008. People got poorer as their assets declined, and as a result they reduced their consumption. They may be only postponing their consumption to see what will happen, but as of the time of writing consumption has stayed low for five years. The decrease in consumption moved the IS curve to the left in figure 6.1. That lowered the interest rate at the intersection of the IS and LM curves, although the economy did not go smoothly from the old equilibrium to the new one. Production changes far more slowly than the interest rate, and that means that the dynamics were more complex than in figure 5.1.

When the IS curve moved left and the interest rate fell, production could not respond immediately to the lower interest rate. To equilibrate the money market the interest rate had to overshoot its eventual resting point at the new equilibrium because it was the only variable that could move fast enough to react immediately to the increase in savings. The level of output could only move gradually up along the new lower IS curve to the point where the goods market is in a new equilibrium, at a lower level of GDP and a lower interest rate. The interest rate rose gradually to its new lower equilibrium level as GDP approached its new lower equilibrium. Production changed slowly and in a single direction. The interest rate changed quickly and overshot its new equilibrium, first falling quickly and then rising slowly.

This process works for normal shifts of the IS curve. But the IS curve in the US moved left a great distance after the Global Financial Crisis and the adjustments that followed. It moved so far that the new IS curve no longer crossed the LM curve at a positive interest rate as shown in figure 7.1. The dynamics in the last paragraph were even more complex in 2008–09, when the interest rate fell to zero. Investment fell, but the economy could not get to the new intersection of the IS and LM curves because the interest rate could not fall far enough.

If figure 7.1 looks like figure 1.3, that is no accident. Neither prices nor interest rates can be negative. The reason interest rates cannot be negative is that investors would rather hold cash than buy bonds that would give them a negative return (that is, that would cost them money to hold). As a result, monetary policy cannot be used to lower the interest rate by

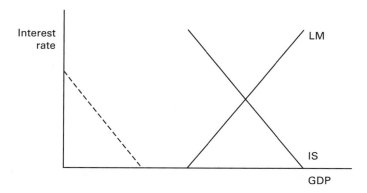

Figure 7.1
The zero lower bound.

expanding the money supply, since the interest rate cannot be made to fall below zero. Monetary policy cannot be used to move the LM curve to the right and move the economy back toward full employment since there is no positive interest rate where the two curves cross. And without an interest rate which can move, we have gone back to the analysis of figure 5.1, where the interest rate is absent.

Keynes observed this situation in the 1930s and drew attention to it in *The General Theory*. In a review of *The General Theory* published in 1936 and in an essay published in 1940, his colleague Dennis Robertson called it a "liquidity trap." At an interest rate of zero, people are indifferent between holding money and holding bonds, and the central bank cannot affect the interest rate by increasing the quantity of money or other means. The IS-LM analysis allows for two macroeconomic policies. Fiscal policy can affect the IS curve; monetary policy changes the LM curve. But movement of the LM curve does not affect the economy as long as the two curves fail to cross at a positive interest rate. Monetary policy does not work in a liquidity trap.

The liquidity trap is represented with an interest rate of zero, but the interest rate typically is just above that level. Short-term interest rates on government obligations can fluctuate narrowly around zero, but other rates stay above that level. Long-term bonds, for example, contain risks in the uncertain future until the bonds come due. Even in a liquidity trap, long-term interest rates have a risk premium and are positive, albeit low. Economists speak of the "zero lower bound," but we should not take that literally for all interest rates.

We also need to recall that the use of straight lines becomes less accurate as movements along curves get larger. The movement into a liquidity trap is a large change, and we acknowledge that figure 7.1 shows only an approximation to the actual condition. The graph explains how the interest rate can fall to zero, but it is less useful in showing how far the IS curve would have to move to lift the interest rate from this floor. Some current Keynesian economists have drawn figure 7.1 with an assumed equilibrium at a negative interest rate. This is logically correct, but it ignores the constraint that the interest rate cannot fall below zero. We can use figure 7.1 with confidence to explain our current condition, but we must use caution when using it to promote specific policies.

This is the position which the economy is still in at the time of writing.. The return on safe assets—that is, bonds issued by reliable governments, such as the United States, Great Britain, and Germany—is essentially zero. Higher interest rates on other assets indicate the risk that lenders incur in making loans to people or governments in Southern Europe who may not pay their debts under some conditions. Monetary policy, increasing the quantity of money, cannot decrease the interest rate any lower than zero, and monetary policy does not work in a liquidity trap.

By contrast, fiscal policy works extremely well. Fiscal policy to increase income is shown in figure 6.1 by a rightward shift of the IS curve. As in figures 4.2 and 5.2, a shift in one curve moves the industry or economy along the other curve. In this case, the movement of the IS curve would normally move the economy up the LM curve. Income and the interest rate would both increase. The rise in the interest rate would reduce desired investment, and the eventual rise in income would be less than the movement of the IS curve. This is what Hopkins claimed in the Macmillan Committee, although he implicitly assumed a vertical LM curve.

If, however, the economy is in a liquidity trap, as shown in figure 7.1, where the IS and LM curves do not intersect, then the interest rate does not change. It is stuck at zero, and any rightward shift of the IS curve will not raise the interest rate from its zero lower bound. As a result, the increase of income will be as large as the shift in the IS curve. There will be no crowding out. Observers who say fiscal policy does not work think only of figure 6.1; they do not realize that figure 7.1 is the correct one to use in a liquidity trap.

Proponents of austerity, however, refuse to contemplate fiscal policy. Countries with large public debts are called on to reduce government spending, not increase it, to pay their debts. Countries with surpluses and countries for which figure 7.1 is still relevant are acting in the same manner. The Western world is fixated on the policy of austerity.

We hear a lot about monetary policy today because fiscal policy, which could be used to increase production and expand employment, has been ruled out for political reasons we will explore more when we consider open economies. People therefore have looked to central banks to reduce unemployment. Central banks in the United States, in Britain, and in Japan have responded with what is now called "quantitative easing." This term describes a monetary policy that is implemented by changing the quantity of money, but it describes the kind of monetary policy that is used when the economy is in a liquidity trap. Since monetary policy normally works by moving the LM curve and lowering the interest rate, how does quantitative easing work?

The answer is that quantitative easing does not work very well. It is meant to work by having the central bank buy longer-dated government bonds, thereby raising their price and pushing down the longer-term interest rate. In the normal conduct of monetary policy, the central bank buys shorter-dated government bonds and thereby pushes down the short-term interest rate. But in a liquidity trap, the short-term interest rate cannot be pushed down any further. The reduction in the longer-term interest rate brought about by quantitative easing is meant to stimulate expenditures and expand the economy in this unusual case.

It is beyond the scope of this book to explain why this might work; it requires thinking about a world in which the price of long-term bonds can move independently of the price of short-term bonds—something Keynes had deliberately avoided thinking about. It is enough here to remind readers that, if monetary policy cannot affect the short-term interest rate, the Keynesian point that you cannot push on a string is basically correct. Quantitative easing has not had much of an effect on unemployment in the United States or in Europe. It is being undertaken because, if there is a liquidity trap and governments are unwilling to undertake expansive fiscal policies, then quantitative easing is all that is left for policy makers to do.

Returning to the Macmillan Committee, we can see that Keynes had a good answer to Hopkins on why expanding government expenditures did not have to be opposed by a reduction in private spending. As in our figure 6.1, a shift of the IS curve to the right moves the economy up the LM curve and may be expected to raise the interest rate. The higher interest rate will discourage investment spending, as Hopkins claimed. But this is a two-step process, as was true in the analysis of the gold standard which Keynes had presented to the Macmillan Committee. This crowding out happens only if the interest rate rises when government spending rises, something the central bank can prevent. And crowding out can't be complete until the LM curve is vertical, when the demand for money is not affected by the interest rate. That was true under the Quantity Theory of Money. But Keynes had replaced this theory with his description of liquidity preference.

A rise in interest rates is possible in a fiscal expansion, but is not likely to happen when the economy is depressed. As described here for conditions after the Global Financial Crisis of 2008, if the IS curve has shifted left so far that it does not cross the LM curve at a positive interest rate, then the interest rate is stuck at its zero lower bound. If government spending rises, this will have no effect on the interest rate until the IS curve moves far enough to move the intersection of the IS and LM curves into positive territory. Until that time, figures 5.1 and 7.1 are the relevant figures, and Hopkins is wrong. Hopkins was incorrect in 1930 when he claimed that crowding out would eliminate rather than reduce the effect of fiscal policy. He was completely wrong in 1936, when Keynes published *The General Theory of Employment, Interest and Money*, and he is completely wrong today.

The collapse of the world economy in the early 1930s plunged Europe and the United States into hard times. Currency crises in Germany, Britain, and the US in 1931 led to restrictive policies that turned a recession into the Great Depression. Life was easier in Britain after it left the gold standard in 1931, but both Germany and the United States continued to experience high unemployment until 1933, when leadership changed in both countries. Adolf Hitler became chancellor of Germany in January and moved swiftly to expand the economy. Of course, he also abandoned democracy for a vicious, anti-Semitic dictatorship. Franklin Delano Roosevelt became president of the United States in March, and he too reversed existing economic policies. He observed the rules of democracy and submitted a set of bills to Congress that are known collectively as the New Deal. His statements and actions changed expectations, and the New Deal led to an uneven recovery. Amazingly in hindsight, some prominent contemporary observers could not differentiate between these two leaders in the first few years in office.

Writing *The General Theory of Employment, Interest and Money* provided Keynes with the argument he needed to answer Hopkins' insistence that an increase in public expenditure would crowd out private investment in an economy at less than full employment. The analysis in *The General Theory* makes it clear that if monetary policy is sufficiently loose to mean that crowding out will not happen through a rise in the interest rate, an increase in public expenditure will cause output and employment to increase. That will cause savings to rise, and in an economy with the public sector it also will cause taxes to rise. Income will rise to the point at which the rise in private-sector savings, coupled with the rise in taxes, is just as large as the initial increase in public expenditure. There need be no crowding out.

Keynes' objective in the period 1937–1940, as war loomed and then began, was to deal with an emerging excess demand for labor, not unemployment. He hoped to make internal balance possible and to make sure that inflation would not be the means of paying for the war, as it had been in the First World War. He did not want the war to be fought with tight money that would benefit the rentier class. Some other way to reduce internal demand in order to release the resources required for the war effort was needed. This gave rise to his book *How to Pay for the War*.

This clear application of Keynesian economics explained Keynes' plan for compulsory savings, or—what is the same thing—forced reductions in consumption. The effect of this proposed plan can be seen by using figure 5.2 to represent Keynesian policy of forced savings for private consumption; figure 5.3 then reveals the impact of wartime government expenditures. Keynes attempted to calibrate the extent of forced savings to balance the effects of the British government's wartime spending so that the government did not have to borrow to finance its efforts. If the government did not increase its borrowing, interest rates should not increase. In fact, Keynes explained that he presented his plan precisely in the hope of averting such a rate increase. And in this condition, the Keynesian Cross was the appropriate tool.

Keynes used the Keynesian Cross because he was analyzing how the economy would work if his plan to keep the interest rate from rising was adopted. His purpose was prescriptive, not descriptive. In addition, he divided spending in a new way. Instead of separating consumption and investment, he separated military and civilian spending. The message was the same. The economy would work best when the demand for the national product was equal to the supply.

Keynes' plan was implemented only to a small degree, but the discussions of Keynes' plan led to Keynesian macroeconomic management becoming firmly established in Whitehall in 1941. The Treasury had been dominated by a Hopkins-like pre-Keynesian view of what makes for responsible policy: that if the government's non-war deficit were to be balanced, private savings would be forthcoming to finance the war effort. It is hard now to understand how anyone could have thought this. Keynes' alternative view quickly came to dominate.

According to Keynes' alternative view, it was necessary to compute the likely economy-wide level of demand for goods and make sure that there would be no inflationary gap between it and overall supply in the economy. Discussions about domestic macroeconomic policy and the need to reach internal balance led to Keynes being taken into the Treasury as an advisor. Although he never held a paid job there, he quickly became the Treasury's effective leader. He used that position to as a base from which to carry out his role in all of the international economic discussions that we are about to discuss.

The General Theory of Employment, Interest and Money did not deal with the second of the problems identified above in our discussion of Keynes' presentations to the Macmillan Committee about the international setting of policy making: How should an economy like that of

Britain in 1930 deal with rising unemployment when the economy is insufficiently competitive internationally? Any increase in public expenditure of the kind that Keynes was advocating to Hopkins would only make the international position worse. Something else is necessary if that problem is to be dealt with at the same time as ensuring that unemployment is dealt with.

Keynes could not immediately turn to dealing with this wider set of problems about the international economy. Immediately after he finished writing *The General Theory*, Keynes had a nearly fatal heart attack. From 1937 on, he focused on the problems that emerged as Britain neared full employment and began its preparations for war. Of particular importance was the need to create room for re-armament without running into inflationary or balance of payments pressures. Policies were needed to reduce *domestic demand* to what was available after the needs for the war effort and trade had been met. This set of issues was about ensuring both internal balance and external balance for the economy.

The Nazis' expansionist plans resulted in a war that dragged on for five years and caused untold suffering around the world. Policy makers in the United States and in Britain remembered the dreadful aftermath of the First World War and began to try to come up with a better plan for conduct of economic policy after the end of this war. Negotiations in the early 1940s culminated in the grand 1944 meeting at Bretton Woods that led to the creation of the International Monetary Fund.

Keynes had many bright, intuitive ideas about the analysis of economic problems of the 1930s that we have been describing, but he lived much too busy a life to work out much of the relevant theory for himself. He may have had the wrong sort of mind for that, and he may have recognized that limitation. He compensated by gathering a group of clever, technically minded young people into the Circus to carry out the formal analysis for *The General Theory*. As a result, Keynes was able as a result to alter both economic policy and economic theory.

But what framework did Keynes have available with which to carry out this international analysis? Very early on, Keynes saw that he needed two kinds of policies to achieve the two objectives of internal and external balance. In order to achieve internal balance, he needed policies to reduce domestic demand to what was available after allowing for the needs for the war effort and for trade. This was the problem of balancing civilian and military spending that Keynes addressed in *How to Pay for the War*. And he also needed policies to obtain a balance of external accounts consistent with the war effort. The first of these needs could be analyzed using the tools Keynes had developed in *The General Theory*. The second required that he return to the difficulties of an economy open to international trade that he had discussed at the Macmillan Committee, and the tools of analysis he had been developing in his *Treatise on Money*.

The setting in the *Treatise* is not that of a closed economy (as in *The General Theory*); it is the international system, a system of the kind that Keynes described and analyzed at the Macmillan Committee. The *Treatise* contained a discussion of the need for both separate national monetary autonomy in the face of difficulties facing individual countries and also an analysis of the need for a uniform international monetary standard that would stabilize the global price level and the global economy. In the final chapter of the *Treatise* there is a discussion of the possibility of fulfilling these needs.

Keynes did not understand how to use this framework when he was talking to the Macmillan Committee. As we have seen, *The General Theory of Employment, Interest and Money* dealt with Hopkins' criticism that fiscal expansion would lead to crowding out. It had provided Keynes with the tools for thinking about internal balance. But the open-economy problems that Hopkins had raised—those having to do with external balance—remained to be dealt with.

8

Bretton Woods and the Swan Diagram

At the beginning of the Second World War, the need for wartime external balance in Britain imposed two requirements that differed according to their time frame. In the short run, just as under the gold standard, there was a financing need. The level of imports required for survival (both military and non-military) had to be paid for somehow. The conversion of a large proportion of Britain's export trades to the production of armaments made this impossible. The country became dangerously dependent on the United States for its short-run survival as a result of Britain's commitment in the summer of 1940 to "victory however long and hard the road may be." The process of engaging the United States in this need led to Churchill's famous letter to Roosevelt of December 8, 1940, and to Roosevelt's generous response in the form of Lend-Lease. This was announced on December 17, 1940 "in the homely image of lending a neighbor a hose to put out a fire." As a result of Lend-Lease, Britain was able to fight the war without the kind of daily threat of financial crisis that had characterized the First World War.

The desire for long-run external balance meant that the economy needed to become competitive again after the war in a way that had not happened after the First World War. Keynes' long-run strategy was to save enough external and financial strength for Britain to preserve its ability to regain in time a satisfactory external position. Keynes aimed to establish a policy framework that allowed individual countries like Britain to promote high levels of employment and output by means of demand management policies, mainly in the form of fiscal policy. This would, it was hoped, avert slumps in growth and would prevent the re-emergence of the kind of global depression that had occurred in the 1930s. Each country would pursue internal balance.

Once he had applied the lessons of *The General Theory of Employment, Interest and Money* to British wartime domestic policy in *How to Pay for the War,* Keynes returned to the lessons he had expressed in *The Economic Consequences of the Peace.* He had put his interest in the international economy on hold as he worked out his theories for closed economies. But Keynes clearly had not forgotten the difficulty he had encountered when trying explain the operation of the gold standard to the other members of the Macmillan Committee. Now that he had solved his closed-economy problem, he could return to his original interests in assuring that countries could remain in both internal and external balance, that they could be prosperous domestically in a world economy.

Keynes' first step was contained in a plan he put forward for a new postwar international monetary system in late 1941 that was designed to make such global full employment possible with the aid of what he called a "Clearing Union." His plan drew on the theoretical arguments in his *General Theory,* and also on the harsh practical example provided by Britain's return to the gold standard in 1925. He was concerned that a shortage of global lending to countries in balance-of-payments difficulty might trigger global malfunction in the form of a global recession. He feared a series of currency crises like those of 1931. This fear also was displayed in 2012 in the difficulties of borrowing experienced by many European countries.

Keynes wanted a global monetary system in in which international money would be sufficiently accommodating. His global Clearing Union was to be something like the clearing system within a national banking process that would meet global liquidity needs without any international risk and without any hindrance or restraint. Keynes wanted this to happen at a low level of global interest rates, and this proved to be a major stumbling block in the negotiations that he had with Harry Dexter White of the US Treasury between 1942 and 1944, in the run-up to the Bretton Woods Conference.

Keynes believed that the mechanism of the gold standard could be both too expansionary as well as too contractionary. His reasons for this are relevant today. The European Monetary Union has features similar to those that concerned Keynes because separate countries have fixed exchange rates between them in the manner of the gold standard. Not only has this system forced countries in the European periphery to have excessively contractionary policies since the onset of the European crisis. It also meant that policies in these countries were excessively expansionary in the period before the crisis in a way that Keynes thought was possible.

The need for something different from the gold standard was discussed in much detail over the next two years with White and others from the

United States. Keynes had argued since the 1920s that the gold standard was broken, and he now understood more clearly why this was so. He had claimed in *The General Theory* that wage and price adjustments did not work well; he had argued at the Macmillan Committee that they did not work fast enough or well enough to be a useful part of the short-term international adjustment process. Keynes reiterated that the attempt to use wage and price flexibility had resulted in conflict and chaos in the interwar period.

This first failing of the gold-standard system created a second one. At the same time as recession was spreading from the export trades, the gold-standard rules of the game required that monetary policy should raise the interest rate and deliberately augment the depression. This was, Keynes thought, no longer practical politics for the postwar world. He had argued at the Macmillan Committee that it was not practical politics for prewar Britain; the gold-standard mechanism should be prevented from working in this way. His Clearing Union proposals were designed to present an alternative. Many are arguing today that adjustment in Southern Europe will only come when this problem is solved for Southern European countries now in difficulty within the European Monetary Union.

Keynes argued that the first, short-run, component of the gold-standard mechanism is likely to be destabilizing in these circumstances. Countries suffering external shocks and experiencing a spreading recession would be likely to come under political pressure to suspend membership of the gold standard. Capital holders would take fright at this possibility and capital would thus tend to flee those countries that experience negative external shocks, rather than cushion the adjustment of such countries to these shocks. Keynes was beginning to produce ideas about self-fulfilling speculative attacks and financial crises. There are parallels with what is happening in Europe today.

Keynes and Britain here ran up against a sting in the tail of Lend-Lease—the "fire hose" that Roosevelt had provided for Britain. A "Consideration" at the end of Article VII of Lend-Lease had stipulated that the United States would have the right to determine the institutional structure of the postwar world in return for donating resources through Lend-Lease. In effect, it was proposed that Lend-Lease would give the United States complete control over the form of Britain's long-run rehabilitation. The United States would be able to determine the conditions under which Britain could recover the export markets it had abandoned during the war.

Using their new-found power to control their old imperial masters, the American firefighters were determined to impose tough conditions.

Roosevelt was determined to dismember the British Empire, as was Secretary of State Cordell Hull. There were many reasons for this wish; it was not just a moral argument. There was a push for markets, a belief that Britain was by then a spent force, a hope by New York bankers to exert ascendancy over London, and an ideological belief in free trade. It became a war aim of the United States that imperial preference should be dismantled.

Britain's free trade area with the Commonwealth countries—Canada, Australia, New Zealand, and South Africa—had been supported by trade preferences since the 1930s. The United States wanted to end these trade preferences and in addition to deny Britain the use of any balance-of-payments restrictions that the competition for Britain's former imperial markets might make necessary. There was a fundamental contradiction in these requirements.

Keynes came to see that there was no way to escape from the sting contained in Lend-Lease since the war against Germany had been inescapable. Britain was a borrower, and it would have to repay the loan. Roosevelt had taken care not to structure Lend-Lease as an explicit loan, and the obligations were not spelled out. They however were clear; Britain would have to live in the world the United States would dominate after the war.

Keynes foresaw that the best way out of this impossible contradiction for Britain was to remake the world economic system. Suppose that free trade were to be imposed on Britain along with open international finance. Then the position of Britain could only be maintained if world trade was free and international finance was managed on a global basis. Britain faced the postwar prospect of having to deal with the United States that was likely to act in protectionist manner in defending its own industries, even though its rhetoric supported free trade. The United States also had the financial power to prevent Britain from being protectionist and to require Britain to abandon the protectionism it had embraced since 1931. This was a grim economic prospect for Britain. It is no wonder that Keynes sent James Meade away one weekend in 1942 to produce a draft document on how to set up an international trade organization.

Two years later, in a particularly tedious meeting at the Board of Trade, Keynes sketched a plan on the back of an envelope and passed it to Meade, remarking that at last he was convinced that he knew how the world economic system should be remade. Keynes listed four goals of international economic policies down the left side of his sketch. The first two goals were short-term; the other two were long-term. There was a policy instrument for each goal, since four instruments were needed to achieve four goals, and there were separate organizations to operate each of these instruments. The first organization, concerned with domestic balance, was national; all the others were international.

The first goal was full employment. This was national, representing balance within each country. The aim was to have full employment without inflation, a condition we call internal balance. Since the goal was national, the organizations to make policies to achieve the goal were national as well. The Employment Act of 1946, revised and expanded in the Humphrey-Hawkins Full Employment Act of 1978, enjoined the US government to reach this goal.

The second goal was adjustment of the balance of payments. This, and the goals that followed, were international. The institutions to accomplish these goals had to be international as a result. Keynes anticipated a set of pegged rates that could be adjusted from time to time as needed. This became the basis of the *Bretton Woods System* after the war ended. The *International Monetary Fund* (IMF) was established as an institution that would help nations adjust their exchange rates, advise them when adjustments were needed, and deal with crises that could occur if adjustments were delayed. The IMF—an improved version of Keynes' Clearing Union—eventually became a crucial policy-making institution.

Keynes' third goal was the promotion of international trade. He hoped that tariffs would be reduced after the war to promote trade. Since the Americans were determined to dismantle the British trading system of the 1930s, Keynes hoped that free trade around the world would provide opportunities for Britain and other countries to prosper. The international trade organization that Keynes proposed to Meade, now known as the World Trade Organization, pursues this goal in a series of international negotiations designed to lower trade barriers.

Finally, Keynes returned to his concerns in *The Economic Consequences of the Peace* for the promotion of economic development. He had maintained his interest in this goal for a quarter of a century and wanted to establish an organization to promote it through international lending. He proposed that a World Bank would complement the IMF among the new institutions. The IMF would deal with short-run macroeconomic problems, while the World Bank would work to promote investment in support of long-run growth. He hoped that the prosperity that came from international growth and specialization would enable the European conditions before the First World War that he had described in chapter 2 of *The Economic Consequences* to spread throughout the world.

In the decade or so since he was writing *The General Theory*, Keynes had incorporated macroeconomic thinking into his framework. No longer would he struggle against Marshall; instead he was firmly asserting that several markets had to be in equilibrium in order for the economy to be in equilibrium. Building on Hicks' IS-LM system, but well before Samuelson's neoclassical synthesis, Keynes had become comfortable with the new field of economics he had created. His objectives were multidimensional. Having understood what he was doing, Keynes came to see that for a single economy one needed to consider not just the market for domestic goods, and the need to achieve full employment, that is, internal balance. One also needed to include the international trading market (the balance of payments) and the need to achieve external balance (that is, a satisfactory balance-of-payments position).

The first two goals of his note make this clear. Keynes then went on to increase the number of countries to more than one. He saw that with two countries, one would want to achieve internal balance in both of the countries and external balance between them (that is, a satisfactory balance-of-payments position between them). It would take economists many years to figure out how to do this analytically, but Keynes leapt to this next step intuitively. In developing his new model, Keynes continued his procedures from the early 1930s, sending messages to his colleagues and students, as he had done in the Circus, and letting them work out the details. The big difference was that he now understood more thoroughly what he was doing and could send more complete messages.

Keynes died shortly after the war ended, and this model of international macroeconomics was not written down until 1952. Meade published it in his book, *The Balance of Payments*, for which he was awarded the Nobel Prize. Meade had played an important part in Keynes' invention of the model, and he described his work as one that "does not claim to make any significant contribution of original work in the fundamentals of pure economic analysis" and has "indebtedness to the ideas of Lord Keynes too obvious to need any emphasis." This model became easy to grasp as a result of the Swan diagram, set out by Trevor Swan in the 1950s, but it did not come into popular use until the 1980s.

The Swan diagram shows how the exchange rate necessary to ensure external balance and the domestic macroeconomic policy necessary to ensure internal balance are jointly determined. Keynes saw that domestic macroeconomic policy influences the external position of the economy; a more expansionary policy raises the level of demand and output and also the level of imports. The exchange rate similarly influences the level of domestic economic activity as well as influencing the external position of the country, and it can move a country toward or away from internal balance. They have to be thought about together.

This, of course, is one of the lessons we drew from Hume's price-specie-flow model in chapter 1. We noted there that Hume assumed full employment implying that rises and falls of the real exchange rate had symmetrical effects—the one causing deflation and the other causing inflation. But in a Keynesian analysis, the opposite of inflation is unemployment. Deflation is no longer possible when wages are sticky. The Swan diagram is a modern way to look at what Hume described in his price-specie-flow mechanism.

Keynes described the connection between external and internal balance in *The Economic Consequences of the Peace*, but he could not express it properly in the Macmillan Committee a decade later because he did not understand how to work with a model that included unemployment. Only after *The General Theory* and the IS-LM analysis could Keynes' insight into the effects of external imbalance on the domestic economy be expressed abstractly.

The Swan diagram accomplishes Keynes' goal. It is composed of two relations. The first one is derived from the IS curve by adding a new variable into the analysis of closed economies in figure 6.1. The second one is simply the modern way to think about the price-specie-flow mechanism described in chapter 1. Our analysis has moved from closed economies in chapters 5–7 to open economies in this chapter. We therefore need to distinguish between domestic and foreign demand, and we replace GDP on the horizontal axis with domestic demand consisting of consumption, investment and government purchases.

The vertical axis represents the real exchange rate, that is, the nominal exchange rate times the ratio of prices at home and abroad as described in chapter 1. As we did there, we express the real exchange rate as the value of the home currency abroad, so a decrease in the real exchange rate can be brought about by a depreciation of the currency or by a decrease in costs and prices at home relative to costs and prices abroad. A decrease in the real exchange rate, measured this way, means that the country is becoming more competitive relative to countries abroad.

A country is in internal balance when domestic production is just large enough to fully use all the resources in the economy; that is, when labor is fully employed and inflation is low. The second market is for international payments. It is measured as the balance on current account in the national accounts, and it is roughly equal to exports minus imports. A country is in external balance when exports are just large enough to fully pay for imports so that foreign trade is balanced, allowing for any interest payments that have to be made abroad and for any long-term capital inflow going to the country. A country is in external deficit if exports are less than this, and it is in external surplus if they are more than this.

The Swan diagram shown here as figure 8.1 therefore includes two markets, and it contains two variables. It looks like figures 4.1 and 6.1, having two curves and having quantities on the horizontal axis. The markets are for domestically produced goods and for international payments; the variables are domestic demand and the real exchange rate.

These lines immediately show the most important lesson of the Swan diagram; internal balance and external balance must be thought about at the same time. We drew this conclusion from the price-specie-flow model in chapter 1; now we repeat it again more formally in the Swan diagram as an important lesson of Keynesian economics applied to the international economy. (Other Keynesian models deal with the effects of fixed and flexible exchange rates.) The level of domestic production and the balance on current account clearly are related to each other. The first curve shows that whenever there are higher exports or reduced imports, that is, whenever there is an increase in net exports, this will add to demand for domestic goods and so to domestic production. But higher domestic production increases the demand for imports and worsens the balance of payments on current account from the second curve. So attempts to achieve internal balance by having an appropriate level of domestic production and attempts to achieve external balance by having an

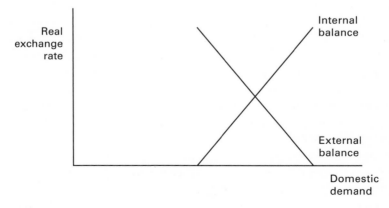

Figure 8.1
Swan diagram.

appropriate level of the balance of payments on current account must be thought about together.

Figure 8.1 shows how to make this interactive adjustment. Consider first internal balance. What happens to domestic output if we start on the line of internal balance, that is, at non-inflationary full employment, and the real exchange rate drops? As this happens, a country's imports become more expensive and fall, while its exports become more attractive abroad and rise. Output would rise if this is all that happens. In order to restore internal balance, domestic demand has to fall enough to offset the effect on output of the rise in exports and reduction in imports; when that happens, to just the right extent, the country will remain in internal balance. In other words, the line that defines internal balance slopes upward. A country has unemployment to the left of the internal balance line and inflation to the right of it.

What happens if we start with external balance and then domestic demand increases? The rise in domestic demand will cause imports to increase; the country will slide into external deficit unless something else happens. But if the real exchange rate drops at the same time, imports will become more expensive and fall, while exports become more attractive abroad and rise. This will tend to offset the worsening external position; if the real exchange rate drops by just the right amount, the external position of the country will remain unaltered. This means that the line that defines external balance has a downward slope. A country is in surplus below the line and in deficit above it.

We put these two lines together in figure 8.1, which looks like a supply-and-demand diagram or an IS-LM diagram. The external balance line is downward sloping, and the internal balance line is upward sloping. Figure 8.1 shows that a country can only achieve both external and internal balance at the point where the two curves cross. To achieve both external and internal balance, it must have the appropriate values for both domestic demand and the real exchange rate.

As figure 8.2 shows, this means that each quadrant of figure 8.1 has a different combination of imbalances. Above the external balance line, the country is in deficit on its current account. To the left of the internal balance line, the country is experiencing unemployment. Deficits have to be financed, and being in deficit means that a country has accumulated foreign debts. These debts can be problematic. The costs of unemployment are not recorded in newspapers and annual reports, as foreign debts are, but they are no less real. Unemployment wastes resources, degrades the work force, and may lead to political troubles. If countries want to be

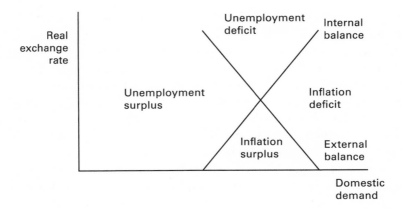

Figure 8.2
Swan diagram with area indications.

in both internal and external balance at the point where the two curves cross, the Swan diagram indicates what policies to follow.

We examine what happens when a country is out of equilibrium by looking first at the possibility that a country could be vertically out of equilibrium, that is, directly above or below it. As shown in figure 8.2, it then would have multiple problems. Being off both curves, it would be experiencing unemployment and an international deficit or inflation and an international surplus. Despite the combination of difficulties, the imbalances can be cured by moving the real exchange alone. Since the real exchange rate is the nominal exchange rate times relative prices, it can be changed either by changing the exchange rate or by changing the level of prices. We discuss this choice extensively later.

A country that is horizontally out of equilibrium faces a similar task. Again, it will be experiencing both internal and external problems, but in different combination than with a vertical displacement. And the policy needed to get to equilibrium is similarly clear; changing fiscal policy one way or the other will do the trick. Monetary policy also could work; changes in monetary policy could be used to bring about the required changes in domestic demand. (If there is full capital mobility, as within the Eurozone today, no single country can affect the interest rate, and monetary policy cannot be used.) Wars typically move countries to the right in figure 8.1 or figure 8.2, creating both internal and external imbalances. Today, as in the 1920s, austerity moves countries to the left, increasing internal imbalances in an attempt to eliminate external imbalances.

Now consider a more complex case. To see what happens when a country is diagonally out of equilibrium, consider the case of a country that is in internal balance but has an external deficit. This country is on the internal balance line up and to the right above where the lines cross. This country needs both a decrease in the real exchange rate and a fiscal contraction. A decrease in the real exchange rate caused either by devaluation or by deflation will increase exports and reduce imports, and therefore will cause domestic production to increase. The fiscal contraction will have to be large enough to offset the expansionary effect on output and make room for the goods that are exported abroad and ensure that the economy remains in internal balance. Lack of coordination of policies will generate either unemployment or inflation. The simple representation by the Swan diagram points to the central problems of macroeconomic policies in open economies. It does this in the same way that the IS-LM diagram points to the central macroeconomic problems of closed economies.

As described in this example, foreign debt can become problematic if investors begin to wonder whether the country will be able to service its debt reliably. Panics all start with the suspicion that some debts may not be repaid. The suspicion about debts gets generalized to a class of national debts of countries in trouble. These countries that were in external balance where investors were willing to buy their bonds, suddenly find themselves out of external balance. If they are in internal balance, they are above and to the right of equilibrium.

Countries subject to the effects of a panic require a combination of policies to resolve their debt problem. The first policy is to reduce domestic spending; this policy is known now as austerity. Austerity on its own moves the country to the left in figure 8.2; the country may well have to move to the left beyond the external balance line and achieve a current-account surplus to begin paying down its debt. As the figure shows, the cost of this policy is unemployment.

How successful will this policy be on its own? It seems unlikely to achieve its goal of reassuring investors and reducing foreign indebtedness because of the costs of unemployment. The growth in unemployment reduces tax revenues, which in turn lower the ability of the government to repay foreign debts. It also triggers government expenditures that may conflict with debt repayment. European history of the early 1930s and again in the last few years suggests that austerity policies intensify the problem of foreign debt instead of reducing it.

The second policy is devaluation. Devaluation on its own will increase exports and reduce imports and will move the country down the graph;

as in the previous description, the country has to move past the external balance line if it is to generate a surplus to repay its foreign debt. As figure 8.2 shows, the cost of this policy will be inflation if it is carried out on its own. This policy therefore will not be successful if devaluation causes inflation to increase so that the real exchange rate does not fall. In that case, the attempt to implement it does not move the country down in the Swan diagram at all.

The indebted country requires a combination of the two policies. Devaluation will increase exports and reduce imports. Austerity—just the right amount—will reduce home demand for goods and leave room for the production of extra exports and the home-produced goods that replace imports. The right combination of policies will move the economy to the intersection of the external balance line and the internal balance line, or even further down the internal balance line into the region of external surplus if the country is to begin repaying its debt. There will be modest temporary inflation as the price of imported goods goes up; such modest inflation will help the country repay its debts, as the real value of its debt is reduced.

To move diagonally in figure 8.1, a country needs two policies; a firmly fixed exchange rate such as the euro does not permit one of them to be used. The indebted countries in Europe are now being forced to try to return to external balance completely through austerity. Since their exchange rate is fixed in the Eurozone, they have to lower prices. They are being placed into Britain's position after the First World War that led to much unhappiness and eventually a general strike. We hope that this history will not repeat itself.

It might seem that external balance occurs only when exports minus imports are zero, but such is not the case. Countries may wish to industrialize by exporting more than they import, using what we called an export-led growth strategy. This is illustrated in figure 8.3, where the dashed line shows the planned export-led strategy in operation. The figure reflects the idea that to achieve an export surplus, an economy will need a more depreciated level of the real exchange rate. It shows that if the depreciation is all that happened, demand for the economy's goods would rise and there would be over-full employment. To obtain the desired export surplus while maintaining full employment, domestic demand must be reduced to make room for the extra exports. Such a policy by some countries may be consistent with a satisfactory global outcome if at the same time other countries wish to industrialize by importing more than they export in order to build an infrastructure of roads, railroads, and schools

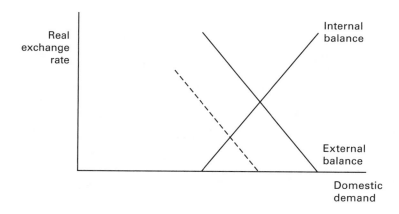

Figure 8.3
Export-led growth.

that promote the growth of industry. By contrast, the circumstances during the early years of the euro did not have this feature. Germany adopted an export-led strategy and other countries in the Eurozone were recipients of German loans. But the loans were not used to build infrastructure of a kind which would support growth, but simply to the buildup of debt. The absence of any plans about what to do about such debt led, after the Global Financial Crisis of 2008, to the problems described here.

Keynes invented the model the Swan diagram explained between 1942 and 1944, and he used it in his discussions with White about the postwar relationships between the Britain and the United States. We employ this model extensively in what follows, and we will show how it can be used to think not just about policies in one country but also about how policy should govern the relationships between countries.

Keynes understood the properties of this model even without writing it down. He argued that there should be as many policy instruments as there were objectives. This requirement would emerge gradually after the war as economists became familiar with Keynesian models, but Keynes stated it clearly in 1944. For one country two goals could only be reached with two policy instruments; for two countries acting together, three objectives (internal balance in both countries and external balance between them) could be reached only with the use of three policy instruments. This was the idea for which Meade won the Nobel Prize.

In addition, long-run and short-run goals had to be considered together. In order for the international economy to be stable, short-run expedients had to be consistent with long-run arrangements. Measures to deal with temporary crises could not destroy the conditions necessary to promote long-run growth, conditions of the kind which Keynes had analyzed in *The Economic Consequences of the Peace*. To be effective, these short-run measures had to bring the world economy closer to its long-run equilibrium. This remains a valuable lesson.

Finally, Keynes had the audacity to envisage new institutions. If the policy levers did not exist, Keynes would create them. He had the intellectual dominance at this stage of his career to envisage remaking the international economy according to the model he had created. This showed an astonishing strength of character. It may be Keynes' largest achievement—and perhaps the one of which he would have been most proud—that the International Monetary Fund, the World Trade Organization, and the World Bank are still operative today. These agencies have been modified many times in the intervening seventy years, but they still fulfill the roles assigned to them by Keynes. In particular the International Monetary Fund has been crucial in protecting the global economy from the effects of financial crises, most recently in the cases of the Asian financial crisis in 1997 and the Global Financial Crisis in 2008.

Why didn't Keynes properly work out the model that underlay his note to Meade? We can only speculate, but it was Keynes' method to send out such messages and let others work out the mathematics. He had used this method in the Circus to produce *The General Theory*, and he clearly hoped to use it again here. Had he lived, perhaps he would have written another book that would have been as innovative and influential as his previous ones. That, however, would have required Keynes to live for many more years after 1944. He was way ahead of his students in thinking of the interconnections between different markets in different countries. It required more than a generation of economists steeped in Keynesian thought to come close to the world model that was anticipated in Keynes' message to Meade. It will require a similar sense of vision to write down the analytic version of Keynes' summary in a way relevant to today's world.

The last speculation gets to the real point. The actual Keynes, as opposed to the hypothetical one just conjured up, was actively involved in making economic policy. Keynes had been working and writing in this area since 1919, when *The Economic Consequences of the Peace* was published. He had spent a quarter-century actively working in this area, with many successes and failures; he was unlikely to have retired from this public arena while he was still able to contribute to it. We must be grateful that his interests were so practical.

9

The Keynesian Age: Crises and Reactions

The decades that followed the Second World War were nothing like those that followed the First World War. The architecture of international economic relations constructed at Bretton Woods provided a format for economic cooperation that led to continuing prosperity. It was a Keynesian age, supported by policies proposed by Keynes throughout the previous quarter of a century.

The International Monetary Fund and the World Bank were the stewards of this cooperation, and the IMF in particular moved into action swiftly to help with postwar adjustments. In an effort to avoid the crises of the interwar years, the Bretton Woods System allowed countries to change their exchange rates for sufficient cause. It was a system of stable-but-adjustable exchange rates, not fixed exchange rates, although Harry Dexter White had insisted that the American dollar be fixed to gold. Britain devalued the pound twice under the Bretton Woods System.

The cooperation stimulated by American generosity in the Marshall Plan was a hallmark of postwar European progress. The European Coal and Steel Community, the Common Market, and other such organizations cemented the practice of cooperation among the countries of Western Europe. They culminated in the Treaty of Rome of 1957, which founded what would become the European Union. This led, in turn, to the European Monetary Union, which introduced the euro as a common currency for eleven members of the European Union in 1999.

Trade promoted economic growth in postwar Europe because the closed economies of the interwar years had not yet undertaken the reallocation of resources that was needed to increase productivity. They did not fully exploit their comparative advantage, and they did not end their reliance on domestic agriculture. Before the First World War, participation in international trade promoted industrialization; after the Second World War, trade again promoted economic growth. Once again, as before the

First World War, manufacturing grew rapidly in Germany, and manu-
factured goods were exported in exchange for agricultural goods from
France and from southern Europe. German industrialization was aided
by imports of new technology from the United States.

The rapid growth of technology in the United States appears to have
started before the Second World War, when productivity grew rapidly
even though the economy was depressed. The fruits of these technological advantages became apparent once the depression and the war were
over. Electricity was introduced before the First World War and gradually became more and more widespread. The internal-combustion engine
gave rise to a variety of new activities centered on transportation. The
expansion of suburbia after the Second World War and the production of
an integrated highway system led to increased reliance on automobiles.
Oil was increasingly used in the manufacture of petrochemicals, plas-
tics, and pharmaceuticals, and the spread of antibiotics after the Second
World War was a major step in health care. And the growth of consumer
entertainment—radio, movies, television, recorded music, newspapers,
magazine—made life more fun in ways that were not included in national
income accounting. The new American products were in great demand in
war-torn Europe, but the European Payments Union enabled Europe to
maintain external balance by restricting Europe's access to dollars.

This golden age was Keynesian for several reasons. The rapid growth
of technology, both in the United States and the rest of the world, was
conducive to growth, as it had been in the period before the First World
War and as Keynes had described in *The Economic Consequences of the
Peace*. This technological growth led to a demand for investment and kept
aggregate demand high. Labor moved from agriculture to industry and
from country to city.

The IMF, which Keynes helped to design, was central to the restora-
tion of growth. The Bretton Woods System gave the world a framework
in which it was known that demand would be kept high and countries
would not be forced to deflate if they were uncompetitive, as had been the
case with the gold standard. In addition prices were more or less stable.
So the economy could be managed, and demand could be kept high in
the way described in *The General Theory of Employment, Interest and
Money* and by the IS-LM curves of figure 6.1, without this being made
impossible by inflation. Unemployment was low until 1971.

The World Bank, which was less central than the IMF, facilitated long-
run growth. The World Bank was designed to help re-create the international pattern of productive trade that Keynes had described in *The*

Economic Consequences of the Peace. At first it lent money to make post-war reconstruction possible in Europe, funding investment at a time when private international capital markets would not do so. Subsequently the World Bank lent money to finance economic growth in developing countries, many of which became today's emerging-market economies in Asia and Latin America.

And, consistent with Keynes' 1944 proposals, international capital flows were regulated carefully after the Second World War. In terms of the Swan diagram of figure 8.1, countries remained largely in both internal and external balance. The buoyancy of demand and macroeconomic policies deriving from Keynes' *General Theory* kept countries close to internal balance. Changes in exchange rates—particularly those made by Britain in 1949 and in 1967—helped to keep countries close to external balance.

The Revenue Act of 1964, which President John F. Kennedy had pushed before his assassination, was a Keynesian policy to stimulate employment in the United States. This fiscal stimulus was designed to get the US out of the apparent doldrums of the Eisenhower years, although it was overtaken by more fiscal stimulus from the Vietnam War before its full effect could be seen. Nevertheless, it stands as the preeminent example of Keynesian policies in the United States.

In 1965, President Lyndon B. Johnson intensified the war in Vietnam and simultaneously promoted many domestic reforms. He hesitated to raise taxes in the midst of all these controversial activities and so soon after the tax cut of 1964. The US economy overheated from the new demands made upon its resources, and the current account of the balance of payments went into deficit. In terms of figure 8.1, the United States moved to the right and had domestic inflation and an international deficit, both of which were caused by an increase in domestic demand.

Germany and Japan became more competitive in the 1960s as they caught up technologically with the United States. This meant that the American competitive position suffered not only because of the absence of policy restraint at home but also because the rest of the world was gradually catching up. The United States moved upward in figure 8.1 as a result of declining prices in its trading partners. The postwar dollar shortage turned into a dollar glut.

The resulting US trade deficit created strains on other Bretton Woods countries. Pressure grew in the 1960s for the US to devalue the dollar, but devaluation was hard in view of the dollar's use as a reserve currency and because the dollar was pegged to gold. There was an alternative: Germany and Japan could have appreciated their currencies. However, they were not willing to adopt policies that would make their successful industries less competitive, preferring to maintain internal balance by spending less at home and making room for their export surplus. Politically, they did not see why they should put their industries at a disadvantage to help out the richest and most powerful country in the world, even if doing so would have allowed them to spend more at home.

European countries, led by France, began to convert their dollar holdings into gold in the late 1960s, and the gold backing of the dollar decreased. This pressure threatened to turn into a run on the dollar, and President Nixon acted to forestall that disruption. In the "Nixon Shock" of 1971, he stopped buying dollars in exchange for gold to maintain the dollar's value in terms of gold and imposed a 90-day wage-and-price freeze and a 10 percent tariff. Only the first of these measures lasted. Several abortive attempts to settle on a new set of exchange rates were abandoned in favor of floating exchange rates.

The resulting devaluation moved the United States down in figure 8.1. It corrected the external imbalance, but it made the internal imbalance worse by intensifying American inflation. The policy imbalance in the US led to global inflation and helped cause the oil scarcity of 1973 that sent the prices of oil and other primary commodities skyrocketing. Spending collapsed in the face of general uncertainty, and economic policy could no longer maintain demand in the presence of inflation. Unemployment rose and economic stagnation set in. Economic theory had followed Keynes in focusing on preventing demand shifts, but the high prices of raw materials and the rapid increases in wage inflation were supply shocks. There was no good theory of how to conduct policy in the face of such supply shifts.

Macroeconomics was in disarray. Keynesian theory as presented in the IS-LM curves of figure 6.1 could not deal with this situation. Countries were meant to be either above their equilibrium and experiencing inflation or below equilibrium and experiencing unemployment. They could not be doing both at once.

Keynesian economists responded to this challenge by developing a theory that dealt with supply shocks, something Keynes had not done. (This is no surprise, in view of the depressed conditions in the 1930s when *The General Theory* was written.) The IS-LM analysis was only the demand side of a supply-and-demand framework for the whole economy. They needed an analysis of the supply side. Keynesian economists returned to the Marshallian Cross of supply and demand shown in our figure 4.1, this time regarding the curves as supply and demand for the whole economy. They described these curves as showing aggregate demand and aggregate supply.

Just as Keynes had done in adding the interest rate to move from the Keynesian Cross to IS-LM, Keynesian economists now added prices to the Keynesian model. They started with the IS-LM model illustrated in figure 6.1 rather than the Swan diagram in figure 8.1. In keeping with *The General Theory*, economists who were analyzing policies to cope with "stagflation" (reduced employment in combination with increasing prices, or stagnation and inflation) chose to stay with an analysis of closed economies. They made this choice for convenience in modeling, even though the oil shocks clearly came from abroad.

Figure 6.1 does not have prices on either axis, since prices are assumed constant in that model, and the money supply is assumed constant in deriving the LM curve. If prices rise, then the purchasing power of a constant money supply decreases. A higher price therefore shifts the LM curve to the left and lowers the level of income. The aggregate demand curve slopes downward on a graph with the price level on the vertical axis as shown in figure 9.1. The aggregate supply curve slopes upward because wages are sticky in this model, as in all Keynesian models. A higher price means that prices have risen faster than wages in the short run. As a result, business firms make more profits and produce more. The aggregate supply curve slopes upward as shown in figure 9.1.

This model was used in the 1970s to explain stagflation. In the IS-LM curve of figure 6.1, the economy could have either unemployment

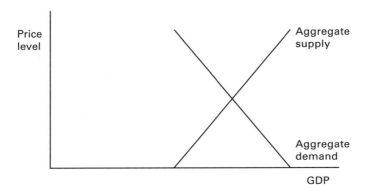

Figure 9.1
Aggregate supply and aggregate demand.

or inflation, but not both. A supply shock that moved the aggregate supply curve in figure 9.1 to the left moved the economy up the aggregate demand curve, reducing employment while increasing prices. The inward shift of the aggregate supply curve came from scarcities of oil and other primary commodities in the 1970s.

Some economists who were skeptical about Keynesian analysis responded to the stagflation crisis in an entirely different manner, arguing that policy makers who attempted to manage demand in the economy tended to aim for too high a level of demand and so cause inflation. They thought that attempts to actively manage the economy should be deliberately abandoned. They argued that aggregate demand would adapt to increases or reductions in aggregate supply. As a result, they focused on the Solow-Swan model (described at the end of chapter 5), in which a country grows rapidly if savings are high and invested, leading to a rapid accumulation of capital. They saw macroeconomic policy as being about encouraging the growth of the supply side of the economy.

The Solow-Swan model worked well in the analysis of long-run economic growth. It did not work as well in analyses of short-run fluctuations of the economy. For example, consider whether shifts in aggregate supply or aggregate demand were more important in the Great Depression. Consider figure 9.1, where the curves represent aggregate demand and aggregate supply. Both prices and output fell in the early 1930s. If aggregate supply had fallen, we would have had stagflation then. It is not possible to explain the Great Depression by a fall in aggregate supply; aggregate demand must have fallen. Even if aggregate supply fell in the 1930s, aggregate demand fell even more. The supply-side story, making use of this growth model, therefore explains only a small part of the Great Depression. Figure 4.2 is applicable if we regard supply and demand as *aggregate* supply and *aggregate* demand. The economy moved from A in 1929 to B in 1933. The economy did not move from A to C in figure 4.2 as the result of a fall in aggregate supply.

Figure 9.1 also can be used to describe the difference between the two kinds of macroeconomics that emerged from the intellectual ferment of the 1970s. Keynesian economists used something like figure 9.1 to argue that policy should be used to insulate the economy from shifts in aggregate demand in order to prevent booms and recessions—including being ready to prevent another Great Depression if that became necessary. Non-Keynesian economists believed that the economy was self-regulating and developed an analysis of the supply side of the economy to support that view. They pointed out that, in the long run, the wage stickiness that

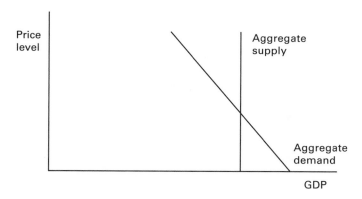

Figure 9.2
Aggregate supply and aggregate demand in the long run.

generates the upward-sloping supply function in figure 9.1 is no longer present, and the aggregate supply curve becomes vertical, as shown in figure 9.2. As a result, it is clear that aggregate supply determines the size of the GDP in the long run. Movements of aggregate demand affect the price level but not the level of GDP. The stock of money is assumed constant in deriving the aggregate demand curve, and increases and decreases in the money stock move aggregate demand and therefore prices. The long-run curves of figure 9.2 re-create the Quantity Theory of Money that was used by Hume!

How short is the short run represented in figure 9.1? It lasts as long as wages are sticky. In figure 9.2, economies are represented in a long run in which we think of all prices being equally flexible. That means, roughly, that figure 9.1 is relevant for economic problems measured in years, whereas figure 9.2 is relevant for economic problems measured in longer periods of time. The problem with using figure 9.2 to explain the Great Depression, as Keynes stated in 1930, is that wages did not become flexible downward in time to avoid a depression. The problem with many macroeconomists today is that they have rejected Keynes and use figure 9.2 for both short-run and long-run problems, rendering them irrelevant at best or misleading at worst when recommending economic policies to deal with current world problems. This is what Keynes meant in the passage we quoted in our epigraph.

10

An International Paradox of Thrift

Inflation was controlled at the end of the 1970s after President Carter appointed Paul Volcker as Chairman of the Federal Reserve System. Volcker dramatically reduced domestic demand with highly deflationary monetary policy. These dramatic events can be analyzed with the IS and LM curves of our figure 6.1, even though they were not billed as Keynesian. Volcker sharply contracted the money supply and shifted the LM curve to the left. That took the United States up the downward-sloping IS curve to higher interest rates and lower employment. It reduced demand, moved the aggregate demand curve to the left, and pushed the economy down the aggregate supply curve in figure 9.1. Inflation returned to low levels.

Something similar happened in Britain with the election of Margaret Thatcher as Prime Minister. Germany had never been an inflationary country and had always had such "discipline"; the spread of these ideas took much longer to spread to the rest of Europe, and elsewhere. Figure 6.1 shows the continuing usefulness of Keynesian tools to such situations, even though the model does not include inflation rates (assumed to be going on in the background) or changing expectations (introduced only informally in Keynesian thought).

The world economy did not return to the status quo ante after the inflationary problem had been resolved. New policies were adopted in developed countries, and Asian countries previously on the outskirts of the world industrial economy moved onto center stage. Capital controls that had been in force during the Keynesian age were relaxed after 1980, making it easy for countries to deviate from external balance. Prices remained largely stable after 1980, however, and the next several decades can be seen as another Keynesian age. The tools described here can help us understand that period.

Japan and later China went from imitation to innovation as they implemented their export-led strategies of economic growth as illustrated in figure 8.3. They moved left from the equilibrium as they became more competitive; domestic demand was adjusted to keep their economies on the internal balance line, and the outcome became one of internal balance with a current-account surplus. Japan used this strategy to raise consumption levels of its citizens to levels previously seen only in Western Europe and in countries populated by emigrants from Western Europe. (Japan ran such an export surplus by consuming and investing less at home than it produced.) China started down this road, and its residents have seen their consumption rise substantially as a result. The difference between these two countries comes not only from the timing of their industrialization, but also from their size. China has an order of magnitude more residents than Japan (1.3 billion versus 130 million today), and its effects on the world economy have been proportionately larger.

China's choice of an export-led policy for growth is particularly important for the rest of the world. When countries seek to grow or to recover from the Global Financial Crisis of 2008 by increasing exports, they increase exports more than imports. An increase in net exports results in capital exports to finance the difference between exports and imports. Capital exports are national savings since they finance production that is not consumed. To rephrase the policies used for growth and recovery, these are policies of increasing national savings. There can be an International Paradox of Thrift analogous to the national one. Production of goods in other countries falls as demand is diverted to China. Output and income fall in other countries, causing them to buy less from China. The outcome is in danger of causing low global demand, rather than supporting a Chinese surplus.

The effects of the Chinese choices on the United States can be seen in figure 10.1. Tax cuts and wars moved the IS curve to the right after 2000. This would have increased the interest rate as it expanded production, as a similar fiscal expansion in the 1980s had done; however, that effect was not present because the Chinese and other Asian surpluses were pushing the American IS curve back to the left. If the dollar had fallen in the early 2000s, that would have added to exports and reduced imports, keeping the American economy growing after the 2000 "dot com" crash. Instead, the Federal Reserve moved the LM curve to the right, which resulted in lower interest rates than before and kept demand and growth up that way.

The international effects of American economic policy can be seen in figure 10.2. The Chinese moved left from the equilibrium as the Chinese economy became more competitive; domestic demand was adjusted to

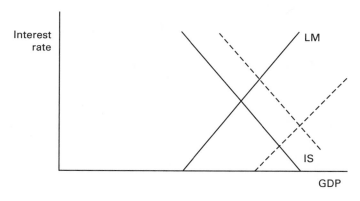

Figure 10.1
The situation in the United States after 2000.

ensure that the Chinese economy remained on the internal balance line, the outcome has been internal balance with a current-account surplus in China, with the Chinese lending money to the United States with which to buy their goods. The United States moved to the right as its international deficit grew. China moved to somewhere like point A in figure 10.2, while the United States moved to somewhere like point B. The International Paradox of Thrift says that if the United States stops dissaving (that is, importing more than it exports) world incomes will fall.

The European Monetary Union was established in 1999 after seven years of preparation. There were initially 11 members of the union that adopted the euro as its common currency; the number has since grown to 17. The establishment of the euro appeared highly successful before 2008 as many member states enjoyed high growth rates in the currency union. Europeans felt that, by establishing a monetary union, they had defended themselves from any re-emergence of the currency turmoil that followed the end of the Bretton Woods system in 1971.

But there were substantial and lasting differences across countries in the inflation of prices and labor costs. The tendency for persistent divergences between euro-area member states was due in part to a lack of responsiveness of prices and wages that did not adjust smoothly across products, sectors, and regions. And this tendency for divergences to grow was due in part to an inadequate European framework for making macroeconomic policy.

The effects within Europe can also be seen in figure 10.2 by changing the countries described. Germany returned to its export-led growth

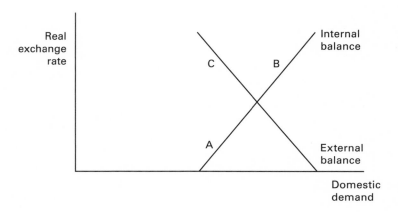

Figure 10.2
The situation in the world as a whole in 2014.

policy. Keynes described it in the nineteenth century, and Japan and China copied it in the twentieth century. It was all too easy for Germany to adopt that old policy in the new macroeconomic framework of the twenty-first century.

The German economy moved left in figure 10.2 from the equilibrium as the German economy became more competitive. Domestic demand within Germany was below internal balance when the monetary union was formed. The resulting low inflation in Germany made it unprofitable to borrow at the interest rate set by the European Central Bank for the European Union as a whole, keeping demand low and so perpetuating low inflation. Domestic demand also was kept low for a number of years by cautious fiscal policy, keeping fiscal expenditure low because revenues were low since income and output were low. A more adequate macroeconomic policy framework in Europe would have acted against this. As a result, by the mid 2000s Germany had attained internal balance and a current-account surplus. Germany lent money to Southern European countries with which to buy German goods.

As the Southern European economies moved to the right in our figure 10.2, they became less and less competitive, even though these economies entered the monetary union in a highly competitive position. The resulting high inflation made it profitable to borrow at the interest rate set by the European Central Bank for the European Union as a whole, keeping demand high and perpetuating high inflation. As in the United States, much of this borrowing financed increases in expenditures on housing. The effect was magnified for a number of years by lax fiscal policy; fiscal expenditure grew rapidly because revenues were rising since income and output were growing so fast. A more adequate macroeconomic policy framework in Europe would also have prevented this from happening.

Germany moved to a point like point A in figure 10.2, while the Southern European countries moved to somewhere like point B. The International Paradox of Thrift, this time within Europe, makes clear that a European recession must result if countries in Southern Europe fail to continue dissaving (that is, importing more than they export). This is happening as we write in 2014.

The world appeared to be awash in savings after 2000. The Chinese pursued their export-led strategy by buying US government bonds to keep their exchange rate low. The US needed to have a fiscal deficit and low interest rates in order to achieve internal balance and ended up with a balance-of-payments deficit. This is shown in figure 10.1, where the IS-LM curves indicate conditions within the country as described earlier. The government's decisions to go to war in Iraq and to cut taxes at the same time shifted the IS curve to the right. But China's export-led growth strategy forced the Federal Reserve to keep interest rates low, despite the fiscal stimulus. The American monetary expansion shifted the LM curve to the right so that interest rates actually fell in what turned out to be an unsustainable boom.

Capital inflows raise the demand for consumption in the importing country. The price of tradable goods in the economy is constrained by the abundant supply of imported goods, while the demand for goods produced at home results in higher prices. This caused an increase in the price of housing. Financial intermediaries took advantage of this profit opportunity to expand their mortgage investments. The innovation of combining loans into tranches with varying risks allowed firms to offer securities of any apparent risk to their customers. It was, in retrospect, a kind of financial alchemy. All this funding flowed into the American housing market, with predictable effects. Housing prices rose to boom levels by the middle of the decade.

The first sign of trouble came when LIBOR (the London Interbank Offered Rate, which is the basic interest rate of the London financial market) jumped dramatically in 2007 and stayed high. The rise came about because of an increase in the risk premium in LIBOR relative to the safe federal funds rate, as investors began to avoid assets that were beginning to seem more risky than advertised. The Federal Reserve reduced its interest rates and began to accept questionable assets in exchange for cash, in order to get reserves into troubled banks. But the year after LIBOR rose was like the Phony War in 1939. Investors tried to convince themselves that nothing was wrong, but the clock was ticking.

The alarm went off in September of 2008. A New York merchant bank, Lehman Brothers, was in trouble. Without the sweetener of government support, Lehman was not saleable, and it was allowed to go bankrupt. This appeared to be a signal that the government was stepping out of the financial collapse; a signal that firms which had taken excess risks in the boom would be vulnerable in the collapse. But hard on the heels of Lehman Brothers' failure came trouble at American International Group (AIG). Although AIG was a multinational insurance company, not an investment bank, it had taken too many bets on what were now toxic assets, and it was about to collapse. The financial epidemic had escaped the mortgage market and infected the whole financial system.

Two days after Lehman Brothers was allowed to fail, the US federal government threw in the towel and nationalized AIG. That only confused the market. Investors could not predict what would come next, and financial markets froze. The end of the housing boom rendered credit ratings irrelevant, as the assumption of independent risks underlying the ratings clearly was inaccurate. "Fire sales" of assets wrecked balance sheets, and the United States went into recession.

European bond markets followed suit. European banks had bought many of the same assets as American banks, and they found themselves unsure of their value. They tried to sell suspect assets as fast as they could, and there were "fire sales" of assets in Europe. Many European governments rushed to sustain their banks by lending them money to help them ride out the panic. Unhappily, the panic then spread to national bonds, which fell in price. The normal expectations of bonds—that they will be serviced without difficulty—changed to an expectation of imminent default. This international transmission of the American crisis made it into a Global Financial Crisis.

The resulting damage has been immense. The world economy is 10 percent poorer than it would have been if growth had continued at the rate before 2007, and unemployment has risen sharply. In many advanced countries the level of activity has not yet returned to what it was in 2007. And the pain is not over yet. No matter how good things get, unemployment is likely to fall only very slowly in the United States and in Europe. For unemployment to begin to fall, we need a resumption of global growth. That does not seem likely under current policies. And growth is also not coming from anywhere else: five years after the collapse, economic growth is slowing in China and in India.

China and Germany are continuing to pursue their export-led growth policy, but United States is reluctant to repeat its earlier consumption boom. The continuing mortgage crisis in the US is keeping consumption low there, reducing Americans' appetite for imports. In Europe, the Southern European counties can no longer absorb large amounts of German exports; instead policies of austerity are forcing reductions in expenditure and so in imports. With all countries trying to save, we are experiencing the International Paradox of Thrift. In such circumstances, incomes have to fall enough to reduce the desire to save for a new lower equilibrium to be reached.

Risks to global growth appear great. There is a continuing risk of a European crisis. There is a widespread wish by both consumers and the financial system to deleverage—that is, to pay down debt. There also is pressure to reduce government deficits and so to pay down public debt. And there is concern about international imbalances. There are imbalances between Germany and Southern European countries, and there is concern about Southern European government debt. There are imbalances between the United States and East Asia, mainly China, and there is concern about the stability of the portion of the United States' debt that is held in the form of Chinese foreign exchange reserves. Owing to this uncertainty, productive investors are holding back from large-scale investments. Many producers apparently think it unwise to invest, just as it seems wise for consumers to save.

How can we get growth to recover and unemployment to fall when there is so much concern of this kind? Depending who you talk with, the unnatural magnitude of either unemployment or national debt is a major sign of disarray. These symptoms of economic distress can be observed in many countries of America and Europe, but these national problems are all parts of an international problem, in fact a global one. Solving the multitudinous national problems will require straightening out the international economy.

Consider the problems that have been caused by countries (among them Germany) that have adopted an export-led growth strategy such as Keynes described in *The Economic Consequences of the Peace*. That strategy preserved internal balance by moving down the internal balance line, as shown on the dashed external-balance line in figure 8.3, or at somewhere like point A in figure 10.2. If Germany were a small country, its being out of equilibrium would not disturb other countries very much. Even though each of the other countries might be a bit out of equilibrium in the opposite direction—up the internal balance line—they would not be unhappy because the effects would be small.

Germany, however, is a large country and a member of the European Monetary Union. In the early twenty-first century, it reprised the strategy that had worked well in the late nineteenth century. Before the current crisis emerged, countries in Southern Europe were necessarily a mirror image of Germany, at point B, and borrowing from Germany. Since Southern Europe was doing this for many years, it accumulated large debts, which Germany now wants it to pay. How can Southern European countries pay those debts?

Keynes gave the answer in *The Economic Consequences of the Peace*, speaking of Germany in the 1920s: "It is certain that an annual payment can only be made by Germany over a series of years by diminishing her imports and increasing her exports … ." Southern European countries can now make payments to Germany only by diminishing imports and increasing exports over a series of years. Figure 10.2 shows the options. Devaluation would accomplish the job if not offset by inflation, as was noted earlier, but countries in the European Monetary Union have adopted the euro and ruled out devaluation. The alternative is austerity— moving to the left in figure 10.2 to point C or beyond. As that figure shows, Southern European countries would have to move left by a large amount in order to generate a surplus sufficient to pay back their loans from Germany.

Austerity is proving a hard road to follow. In addition to the economic problem of contracting a modern economy so much, such a large movement of income is politically problematic. It is not clear that a leftward movement in figure 10.2 large enough to bring Southern Europe beyond external balance is politically possible. Southern European countries moved into surplus territory in 2013, but who will buy the goods of the Eurozone? The austerity is forcing Southern Europe into a recession. It is also creating an International Paradox of Thrift.

Consider figure 10.2 again. The Eurozone as a whole now is at point A. China and Japan are also at point A. At the time of writing in early 2014 Japan has adopted expansionary monetary policy which has caused the yen to devalue, increasing its exports as a path to economic recovery. The United States is already at a point like B in figure 10.2, something which partially offsets the effects of China and Japan being somewhere like point A. Can the US expand to absorb exports from Europe as well? In that case, the Southern European problem might be avoided by Europe exporting to the United States and getting dollars in return. Germany would accept dollars instead of euros from Southern Europe, but it would not have moved from somewhere like point A itself and so would not have done anything itself to help solve the Southern European problem.

Will the United States be willing to absorb exports from Europe? It tried something similar a decade ago when China set out on its path of export-led growth. The results were low interest rates, a housing boom, and the Global Financial Crisis. That does not look very attractive in retrospect. The alternative—devaluing the dollar to avoid increasing imports, leaving Europe in the lurch—is also unattractive. Simple Keynesian tools can expose the major macroeconomic problems of the world today; only politicians can choose how to respond.

The problem of too many export-led countries is a problem of arithmetic. How can every country's positive balance of trade add up to global balance? It also can be seen as an International Paradox of Thrift. Any country, but particularly a small country, can use an export-led growth strategy without adverse effects on the world economy. But when *all* countries try to save, we know from the Paradox of Thrift what will happen. World output will fall, moving people down their consumption function until their savings equal their intended investment. We will relive the 1930s if national economic policies do not change. Even if things do not get worse, the International Paradox of Thrift explains why the recovery from the Global Financial Crisis of 2008 has taken so long. It suggests why, without a change of policies, it is likely to go on being a very slow recovery.

What would a Keynesian recommend to avoid this pessimistic prospect? To restore balance and prosperity to the world economy, only a few countries need alter their economic policies. China, Germany, Britain, and the United States all have international assets or can borrow at low interest rates. They are in the position shown in figure 7.1, which brings them to the policy choices shown in figure 5.1. They should expand domestically, moving to the right in figure 7.1. This would increase domestic consumption—the universal aim of public policies. It also would reduce pressure on deficit countries and enable them to expand their current depressed economies.

Recall the application of figure 10.2 to Europe today. Germany is below the external balance line at point A; the Southern European countries are below it at point C. Germany is there by choice, whereas the Southern Europeans have been forced there by financial pressure. The difference between the two regions is apparent in figure 10.2 in the different levels of the real exchange rate—overvalued in Southern Europe and undervalued in Germany. This is an echo of the interwar years as anticipated by Keynes in 1919. Just as Germany's independence was curtailed by the Treaty of Versailles, Southern Europe today has been curtailed by the Global Financial Crisis.

Something similar is happening globally. Global aggregate supply is above global aggregate demand. Simply relying on a return of private-sector investment to recreate the kind of growth process that Keynes described at the beginning of *The Economic Consequences of the Peace* will not be adequate. And yet many regions of the world are seeking to maintain austerity and expand aggregate demand by growing their exports. This is true of the United States, of Europe as a whole, and of China and the rest of East Asia. Such polices will cancel each other out and will not deal with the International Paradox of Thrift. Until the private-sector demand recovers, more expansionary domestic policies are needed—not just in Europe, but globally. It will be the time to think about reducing debts when that recovery has happened—not now, before private-sector demand has recovered adequately.

We hope that the insights of Keynesian theory and economic history will enable policy makers to resolve international tensions today more easily than their forerunners did in the interwar years.

Glossary of Economic Terms

Aggregate demand   Total demand for goods and services in an economy.

Aggregate supply   Total supply of goods and services in an economy.

Austerity   The current term for fiscal contraction—that is, contractionary fiscal policy, such as cutting government spending.

Bank rate   The Bank of England's discount rate, customarily written without the definite article.

Bonds   Records of loans from purchasers of bonds to the issuers. Only government bonds are considered in this book, simplifying from the great variety of bonds that exist.

Bretton Woods System   The international financial system, based on stable but adjustable exchange rates, worked out by John Maynard Keynes and Harry Dexter White at Bretton Woods, New Hampshire.

Capital   A term that has two meanings in this book. The dominant meaning is the result of investments made by firms and governments which lead to the construction of physical buildings, machinery and other forms of infrastructure; economists call such infrastructure "capital." The other meaning, as in "international capital flows," refers to the difference between a country's exports and its imports. (See the definitions of external balance and international capital flows below.)

Central banks   Banks, normally owned by the government of a country, that are charged with preserving stable prices and full employment. Not to be confused with commercial banks that make loans to businesses and individuals. Examples are the US Federal Reserve System and the Bank of England.

Circus   A group of young economists who discussed Keynesian economics in Cambridge in the early 1930s.

Closed economy   An economy without any foreign trade. To think of an individual economy as a closed economy is a simplification, but the world economy as a whole can be seen as a closed economy, since we do not trade with outer space.

Crowding out   What happens when a rise in government spending is offset by a fall in private spending.

Current account   The part of the balance of payments that is "above the line"—roughly, exports minus imports minus any payments of debt interest abroad. Capital exports, or capital imports are items "below the line"; they are equal to the lending abroad, or borrowing abroad, which results from items above the line.

Domestic demand   The horizontal, quantity axis of the Swan diagram, consisting of consumption, investment, and government purchases. For a closed economy this it is equal to GDP, the horizontal axis of our graphs of the Keynesian system and of the IS-LM model, because by definition there are no exports or imports from or to a closed economy. When we consider open economies, we need to separate domestic demand from overall GDP.

Domestic economy   Economic conditions within a country in an open economy (that is, an economy with trade and international capital flows).

Equilibrium   A position in which all the parties involved are content to stay in this position without moving.

Eurozone   Countries that belong to the European Monetary Union and use the euro as their common currency.

Expectations   Predictions of the future by the parties in economic models. The simplest idea is that expectations are "static"—that businesses and individuals expect existing conditions to continue into the future. Deviations from this simple idea are noted in the text.

Export-led growth   A policy of stimulating economic growth by exporting goods and services for the bonds of importing countries. In other words, businesses sell goods abroad for bonds. A country dedicated to export-led growth thereby exports capital.

External balance   Where trade is balanced, the balance on current account is zero, and exports are equal to imports. (These conditions are three ways of saying the same thing.) Capital outflows—lending abroad—can enable external balance to be attained temporarily in countries undergoing export-led growth in which there are positive net exports; capital inflows—borrowing from abroad—can enable external balance to be attained temporarily in countries in which exports are less then imports.

Fiscal policy   Government policy concerning the level of government spending or taxes. In this book, the focus is on government spending.

General-equilibrium analysis   Analysis of several markets at once, showing the interactions among them.

Golden age of economic growth   The period of rapid growth, particularly in Western Europe, from 1945 to 1973.

Gold standard   A system of fixed exchange rates in which each country maintains a fixed value of its currency in terms of gold and allows the free purchase of gold with its currency.

Gross Domestic Product (GDP)   A measure of the quantity of production of goods and services in a country. This quantity is also referred to as national production or national income. All these terms are used interchangeably in this book.

They differ in how they are calculated and in how taxes are treated, neither of which we discuss.

Hyperinflation   Very rapid inflation, typically defined as 50 percent or more per month.

Internal balance   Full employment of resources and low inflation.

International capital flows   What we have when bonds of one country are sold and held in other countries, typically measured by looking at the current account in the balance of payments. A positive balance (that is, positive net exports) leads a country to lend money abroad—a capital outflow. A negative balance leads it to borrow money from abroad—a capital inflow.

International Monetary Fund (IMF)   An international institution, established as part of the Bretton Woods System after the Second World War, to manage an international monetary system in which exchange rates between countries were fixed but adjustable. The IMF effectively acts like a central bank for the world, lending to countries at times of financial crisis.

Investment   Used generally in this book to mean expenditure on economic output which is used by firms and governments for the construction of physical buildings, machinery and other forms of infrastructure. Occasionally used to refer to the purchase of national bonds.

Joint determination   What we have when two economic variables are determined simultaneously and it is impossible to say that one variable causes movements of the other without acknowledging that the second variable also causes movements of the first one.

Keynesian age   A period of stable prices in which economic policies have the effects that Keynes asserted they would have.

Keynesian Cross   A simple graphical representation of Keynesian economics featuring a savings function and fixed amounts of investment and government spending.

Keynesian unemployment   Involuntary unemployment—that is, a situation when not all people seeking work at the going wage are able to find it.

Liquidity preference   The part of the demand for money that describes the desire of people and business firms to hold money for future purchases of bonds and other securities—a desire to be liquid now to make possible a speculative gain in the future. The size of this demand depends on the cost of holding money, that is, the interest rate. This part of demand is in addition to the demand for money for transactions, which mainly depends on the level of economic activity, not the interest rate.

Liquidity trap   A situation in which the IS curve has shifted so far to the left that it doesn't intersect the LM curve at a positive interest rate, and the interest rate consequently falls to zero.

Long run   A period long enough that all prices are responsive to underlying economic forces rather than to their recent history.

Marginal efficiency of capital   The demand curve for investment as a function of the interest rate.

Model, economic   A simple representation of a complex economic reality that serves to clarify important relationships.

Monetary policy   Open-market purchases and sales of bonds by a central bank that serve to increase or decrease the amount of money available for people and business firms to hold.

Money supply   The amount of money in an economy, determined in the distant past by the amount of specie held in the country and now by the interaction of central banks and commercial banks. Keynes assumed that the central bank determined the money supply by itself, but we now think there are several factors that determine the supply of money.

Multiplier   The extra effects of an increase in government spending which occurs when the initial workers supported by the government spend part of their extra earnings, increasing the earnings of other workers who also spend part of those additional earnings.

National production   Measures of national production of goods and services, assumed in this book to be equal to national income or Gross Domestic Product.

Net exports   Exports minus imports.

Open economy   An economy with foreign trade and international capital movements—that is, an economy that is "open" to the rest of the world.

Open-market purchases   Purchases of bonds and other securities by a central bank to increase the money supply.

Paradox of Thrift   The proposition that everyone cannot increase savings at the same time, because the extra savings will reduce spending in the economy as a whole until savings fall back to their original level.

Price elasticity   A measure of the responsiveness of quantity purchased to the price of a good. Unitary price elasticity is where a rise in the price of a good causes a reduction in quantity demanded which exactly offsets the rise in the price to keep the total expenditure constant. Zero price elasticity is where the quantity is not responsive to the price at all; infinite price elasticity is where the quantity is so responsive to the price that even the smallest change in the price sends the quantity to zero or infinity.

Price-specie-flow model   Hume's theory of how movements of specie keep countries in balanced trade.

Quantity Theory of Money   A theory according to which changes in the money supply change all prices together in the same proportion as the change in the money supply.

Real exchange rate   The product of the nominal exchange rate and the ratio of prices in two countries; it is a measure which allows for the fact that a rise in home prices relative to foreign prices can offset the effect of a depreciation of the exchange rate in cheapening a country's prices abroad. The real exchange rate is measured in this book so that a decrease means that home goods are cheapened abroad in foreign currency. Such a decrease in the real exchange rate makes a country more competitive.

Reparations   Obligations imposed on Germany after the First World War that functioned like German debt to the Allies.

Savings   Income not consumed.

Short run   A period short enough that some prices, chiefly wages, are sticky, that is, more responsive to their previous level than to current economic forces.

Specie   Gold and silver coins.

Sticky prices   Prices that do not change rapidly in response to changes in economic conditions. Keynes typically assumed that wages were sticky and that product prices were not. Economists now define the long run as a period long enough that prices have adjusted to underlying economic forces and sticky prices are not an issue.

Supply and demand curves   Separations of the desires of consumers and producers to show how, taken together, these desires can determine both the price and the quantity of goods produced and purchased.

Transfer Problem   To repay its foreign borrowing, a country will have to export more to its creditors than it imports from them. A problem arises if the creditors are not willing to purchase the necessary extra exports.

Unintended investment   Investment, not planned by firms, that shows up in excess inventories and leads to a reduction in production.

Sources and Further Readings

Chapter 1: quotation from David Hume, "Of the Balance of Trade," in *Essays: Moral, Political and Literary* (1752); Kevin H. O'Rourke and Alan M. Taylor, "Cross of Euros," *Journal of Economic Perspectives* 27 (3): 167–1992 (2013)

Chapter 2: quotations from John Maynard Keynes, *The Economic Consequences of the Peace* (Macmillan, 1919); Robert Skidelsky, *Keynes: A Very Short Introduction* (Oxford University Press, 2010)

Chapter 3: quotations from John Maynard Keynes, *Activities 1929–1931: Rethinking Employment and Unemployment Policy, Collected Works of John Maynard Keynes*, volume XX (1981); Peter Temin and Gianni Toniolo, *The World Economy between the Wars* (Oxford University Press, 2008); Barry J. Eichengreen, *Globalizing Capital: A History of the International Monetary System* (Princeton University Press, 2008)

Chapter 4: Michael Thompson, *Rubbish Theory* (Oxford University Press, 1979)

Chapter 5: John Maynard Keynes, *The General Theory of Employment, Interest and Money* (Macmillan, 1936); quotation from Truman Bewley, *Why Wages Don't Fall in a Recession* (Harvard University Press, 1999); Roger E. Backhouse and Bradley W. Bateman, *Capitalist Revolutionary: John Maynard Keynes* (Harvard University Press, 2011)

Chapter 6: Lance Taylor, *Maynard's Revenge: The Collapse of Free Market Economics* (Harvard University Press, 2010); Nicholas Wapshott, *Keynes Hayek: The Clash That Defined Modern Economics* (Norton, 2011); Warren Young, *Interpreting Mr. Keynes: The IS-LM Enigma* (Polity, 1987)

Chapter 7: Paul Krugman, *End this Depression Now!* (Norton, 2012)

Chapter 8: Benn Steil, *The Battle of Bretton Woods: John Maynard Keynes, Harry Dexter White, and the Making of a New World Order* (Princeton University Press, 2013)

Chapter 9: Barry J. Eichengreen, *Exorbitant Privilege: The Rise and Fall of the Dollar and the Future of the International Monetary System* (Oxford University Press, 2011); Judith Stein, *Pivotal Decade* (Yale University Press, 2010)

Chapter 10: Menzie D. Chen and Jeffrey A. Frieden, *Lost Decades: The Making of America's Debt Crisis and the Long Recovery* (Norton, 2012); Peter Temin and David Vines, *The Leaderless Economy: Why the World Economic System Fell Apart and How to Fix It* (Princeton University Press, 2013)

Index